Christmas
in All
SEASONS

Christmas
in All
SEASONS

Geneva M. Butz

United Church Press
Cleveland, Ohio

United Church Press, Cleveland, Ohio 44115
© 1995 by Geneva M. Butz

All rights reserved. Published 1995

Printed in the United States of America on acid-free paper

00 99 98 97 96 95   5 4 3 2 1

Library of Congress Cataloging-in-Publication Data

Butz, Geneva M., 1944–
    Christmas in all seasons / Geneva M. Butz.
       p.   cm.
    Includes bibliographical references.
    ISBN 0-8298-1068-4 (alk. paper)
    1. Christmas—Anecdotes.   2. Church year—Anecdotes.   3. Christian life—
Anecdotes.   4. German Reformed Congregation (Philadelphia, Pa.)—
History.   5. Philadelphia (Pa.)—Church history—20th century.   I. Title.
BV45.B85   1995
242—dc20
                                                                95-16995
                                                                    CIP

To Francis of Assisi,
whose teachings live on

Contents

Contents

Lent

Easter

Pentecost

Preface

This book is dedicated to Francis of Assisi, creator of the first Christmas creche, who once urged the church to "Preach the gospel at all times. If necessary, use words."

That's what Francis was doing when he set up the first Christmas creche in the year 1223 at the grotto of Greccio in Italy. He wanted to make the humanity of Jesus more accessible to the people of his day. He used the creche and the animals to call people back to their basic humanity and unity with all creation through the very humble birth of Jesus. It is Francis's insight into preaching, his voice, that we hear coming through our urban Christmas creche at Fourth and Race Streets in Philadelphia, Pennsylvania.

"Preach the gospel at all times. If necessary, use words."

The stories in this collection tell of the kind of preaching the congregation of Old First Reformed Church, United Church of Christ, does in Center City, Philadelphia. They are authentic stories, congruent with the gospel. A newspaper reporter told me recently, "What makes your church's Christmas creche really speak is that you make room inside your church building for the homeless."

"Preach the gospel at all times. If necessary, use words." Francis's advice is still worthy of our consideration.

Acknowledgments

I would like to thank Ed and Shirley Beers, Krystyna Gorniak, Joanna Robinson, and Tim Schramm for their thoughtful reading of the stories in manuscript form. I am also grateful to Rosemary Polo and Robert Wright for their technical assistance with the computer that they offered so graciously, even when time was at a premium. My special thanks go to Marion M. Meyer for her constant support and encouragement in writing the manuscript and for her helpful suggestions for improving it. And to the people of Old First Reformed Church, I express my admiration for their willingness, year after year, to offer the living Christmas creche as their special gift to the people of Philadelphia.

Introduction

A Church for All Seasons

Animals at Fourth and Race Streets in downtown Philadelphia? What was once a startling innovation has become a Philadelphia tradition. Begun in 1973 by then pastor Reverend H. Daehler Hayes, the live-animal Christmas creche at Old First Reformed Church, United Church of Christ, is known throughout the city. Many families make an annual pilgrimage to see the animals, remembering the first time they stumbled upon the creche by accident. And they bring their friends and out-of-town guests too.

Old First has become known as "that church with the animals at Christmas time." Even the news media have picked up on the public's interest in our nativity scene. One Christmas Eve a local television station set up cameras near the stable so that the weather reporter could give the forecast direct from the creche. Some years we have even made the nationally syndicated news wires. Clippings have been sent to the church from as far away as Boston, Pittsburgh, and Milwaukee.

Normally Mary, Joseph, the baby, the Magi, and the shepherds are portrayed by mannequins that stand outdoors in our church courtyard amid the animals in a makeshift stable for the two weeks before Christmas. But on Christmas Eve church members dress as the characters—and there is always a real baby! After a reenactment of the story using scripture and Christmas carols, everyone is invited indoors for a traditional candlelight service. And Mary, Joseph, the baby, and the others follow as we all move into the large church sanctuary to hear the well-known Gospel readings and sing the familiar carols. One year someone remarked how great it was to gaze at the faces of the church members in costume: "They are real, ordinary people; they look just like we do! They are so interesting and inspiring. Each one looks so different. I was fascinated."

But what continues to surprise us is that for several weeks following Christmas, when the mannequins have been put away for the season and the animals have returned to the farm, people still slow down as they drive past the empty stable on our corner. Some even get out of their cars to take a closer look, hoping to recapture the charm of the animals and the promise of the story. There is something in all of us that doesn't want Christmas to end. We keep our Christmas decorations up as long as possible; we want the hope and joy of Christmas to last the whole year long.

And you know, it does!

After Christmas we don't have to put Christ away with the decorations. The baby grows up and becomes an adult we can follow and learn from throughout the year. Have you ever thought of leaving the infant figure from your creche out until Lent, as a reminder that "God is with us," not only at Christmas time, but all year long?

Following the Christmas season we are introduced to a whole year of "holy days," holidays within the life of the church. Each one is a very special celebration. There's the visit of the Magi, the baptism of Jesus, the transfiguration, and then the journey to Jerusalem and Jesus' death on the cross. Christmas is just the beginning of a story that transcends time and culture. And each part of the story holds within it the possibility of touching our daily lives. Though our secular culture does not celebrate the other events of the story with the same intensity that it does Christmas, the church has a special season for each event in the life of Christ.

The creche is simply the starting point. It invites people to come inside the church and discover more about this baby who grows up to become a very special human being, a unique revelation of God. They are invited to learn that in the church we are part of Christ's family, part of Christ's body, the church. We are baptized into this one body, and become individual members of it.

Old First Reformed Church, in the historic part of Philadelphia, near Independence Hall and the Liberty Bell, is among the oldest congregations in the nation. The first organizational meeting of the German Reformed branch of what is now the United Church of Christ was held here in 1747. Today the church plays an active role in the neighborhood as people come from around the city and region to worship and work with us.

In the pages that follow you will learn of the many ways our church lives out the seasons of the liturgical year. We celebrate these holidays not only by ourselves, but with children from our neighborhood, young people from around the world, the homeless and destitute who come to our doors seeking help, artists who study and teach in nearby schools, visitors who show up for worship on any given Sunday, and people who live and work in the Center City area.

Although almost half these stories are Christmas stories, centered around our live-animal Christmas creche, others celebrate the lenten and Easter seasons, when our church sponsors a citywide competition inviting artists to submit contemporary interpretations of the crucifixion theme. The winning entry is displayed on the outdoor cross for two weeks during Lent in the spot where the creche stands in winter. Still more stories from the life of our congregation take us through the Pentecost season. Truly our church, and every church, *is* a church for all seasons. I hope you will gain insight into the Christian life from these familiar stories as you live them in the pages of this book. And you will find, as we have, that the stories keep on multiplying.

In the end, the message of Christmas is really about salvation. Salvation is God's extravagant gift to each one of us. Jesus, "the one who saves," came into the world that we might have life and have it abundantly. Salvation is that special gift that need not be put away with the Christmas decorations. It is given to each of us the whole year, our whole lives long. Salvation is the gift that we find in the church, now and in every season, and into eternity.

Old First Reformed Church is much more than "that church with the animals at Christmas." It is a way to stay connected with the ongoing story of Jesus who lives and reigns among us in all the seasons of our lives.

ADVENT

Voices from the Wilderness

🌿

I usually think of Advent as beginning with our community Thanksgiving service, which is always held on the Tuesday evening before Thanksgiving Day. For years and years the Philadelphia Boys Choir and Chorale has sung at this celebrative service. The church sanctuary is usually filled that evening. With a program of patriotic and religious songs, the event is quite uplifting and inspiring.

One year, however, the Boys Choir was not able to come. Instead we enlisted the Singing City Choir, another citywide volunteer choir with deep roots in the civil rights movement, dating back to the 1940s. Made up of citizens of all races and backgrounds from around the region, the choir has traveled to Russia and the Middle East as goodwill ambassadors from the United States. Its repertory is quite different from the patriotic music the Boys Choir sings. The Singing City Choir offers folk songs, liberation music, as well as traditional religious compositions. So, for this one year, the mood of our annual Thanksgiving service had been altered.

In addition, we had invited some men from our church's homeless shelter to join us as special guests for this particular service. Arriving early, the men had the best seats in the sanctuary—the first row of the balcony. From this vantage point, they took in everything, and intermingled with people from all walks of life who were in attendance.

Later, one of the men from the shelter stopped me to thank me for the special service of worship. "I especially liked the Israeli folk music the choir sang," he commented. "It reminded me of the people of Israel traveling through the wilderness. And every day God gave the people food to eat. That's what is happening with us. We are in the wilderness, and every day God is feeding us," he added as he looked around at the other guys from the shelter.

When I heard the word *wilderness*, I listened carefully. "Tell me about the wilderness," I urged.

Another man spoke up, a man who had been out on the grate for years. He hides the pain of living in the wilderness by drinking. He was the last person I expected to voice a critical word about his situation.

He spoke quietly, but coherently. "For years, when I was out on the street, I never realized people really loved me. People used to bring blankets and coffee to me on the grate. I would shout obscenities at them. I didn't care. I didn't trust them. I didn't even trust myself. But now that has changed. Now I know that people love me, and most importantly, I love myself."

Another voice from the wilderness came from Carlos, a man who had stayed in our shelter for several months. He was the first to speak one evening at our prayer session. This time Carlos wanted to give thanks. He was happy and exclaimed, "God is always helping me."

Because of his broken English, it was not easy to follow Carlos's conversation. But slowly a story emerged. Carlos began to speak about his life on the street and about his drug habit. "It was so bad," he reflected, "that I didn't care what I did to my body. I was even shooting up dirty water out of the gutter. I could have gotten ill from all those germs. How crazy I was then," he added, as he continued his story.

One day, Carlos told us, he was so hungry he didn't know what to do. He was sitting on the steps of an abandoned house just thinking about stealing a car battery to buy food. But he didn't want to do that. So Carlos said to himself, "If I'm going to eat, God is going to have to give me food."

While he was resting there, still trying to decide what to do, Carlos told us, a priest appeared with two children, and the priest gave him a sandwich. Carlos was so hungry that he immediately began to eat the sandwich. Then he remembered that he had forgotten to thank the priest, so he ran after him. But the priest had vanished and was nowhere to be found. Carlos quickly added, "But I *did* eat the sandwich."

"Now," Carlos concluded, "I always say thank you."

The wilderness is what our world is about. I find that the homeless, those who walk the lonesome pavements of our city day in and day out, have a prophetic word for us out of their wilderness experiences. They remind us that God is the One who feeds us in all the wilderness places of our lives. Their witness also affirms that there is enough bread to sustain life, and more to share with others.

This insight the homeless offer us is a good place for us to begin our Advent journey. As the prophet Isaiah wrote, "See, I am sending my messenger ahead of you, who will prepare your way; the voice of one crying out in the wilderness. . . ."[1] Thanksgiving and Advent—somehow the "thank-you" of one celebration leads into the next, and we find ourselves in the wilderness again, waiting for God to give us the gift of life.

Preparing for Birth

In Luke's Gospel the angel Gabriel visits Mary privately and tells her to prepare, for she is to bear a son who will be called Child of the Most High. Preparing for birth—that is what Advent is all about. A tiny baby arrives to remind us that God is not through with us yet.

One Advent, six of our church families were waiting for a newborn. This was the first time in the eight years I had been pastor of the church that so many women were pregnant. Three of the families were expecting their first child, and the other three, well, they had not planned on another child. These families were very surprised by this sign of God's presence in their lives. They told me this would probably be their last child.

So one week I decided to telephone each mother, and in some cases I spoke to the fathers as well, to learn from them what it is like to prepare for birth. I was glad I talked to them because I've never been pregnant; I don't have firsthand experience of the birthing process. But, in speaking to these families, I discovered that I was "pregnant" too; we were all "pregnant." As we shared in the joy of these six expectant couples, the whole church was in a very real sense preparing for birth. We were getting ready to make room for newcomers in our church family.

The questions I posed to the soon-to-be parents were twofold: How do you feel about the coming baby, and what are you doing to prepare for birth?

To my surprise, only one of the mothers said she was excited by the wonderful news. The other five were not so sure; they were afraid. One mother said that when she heard the news from the doctor, she was in complete shock. She hadn't thought about having more children. A first-time mother said, "I feel the baby is an intrusion. Change will come. I don't know if I'm ready to make the necessary sacrifices."

The fathers were much less apprehensive. One said, "I'm confident. There's no stress." Another, "I'm looking forward to it."

An additional surprise was to learn that not one of these families had prepared a room for the new child. In my inexperience, I would have thought, "A baby's coming—we've got to prepare a room."

One mother-to-be said, "Well, we're thinking about it." Another said her family wanted to look for a new house but hadn't started yet. "I don't know what we'll do," said a third, but then she added, "there's always room for a baby in the house. It will expand the love of the family. We'll find a way." A first-time father believed that "the baby only needs a dresser drawer for the first few months." Another family was concerned that too much preparation might bring bad luck. "We're not even going to think of a name," they added.

But the families were making inner preparations. Every mother spoke about facing changes—bodily changes, anxiety about new responsibility for another human being, and lifestyle changes. One mother said, "Now we have a new direction. I'm thinking about the future. We're talking more with our current children to prepare them emotionally to welcome the new child." A father-to-be told me, "I had dreams about the joy of fatherhood. Now I feel God is saying, 'You're ready! The timing is right.'" Another mother who had been very fearful of a possible miscarriage in the early months now felt ecstatic. "I'm happy to share the joy with others," she said. One woman reported that she gets tired much more easily, another felt relaxed, and a third said she is more emotional. A fourth added, "Christmas is coming, only this year it will be in January."

I enjoyed speaking with these pregnant mothers and fathers, and they seemed to be happy to share their experiences with me too. It's Advent, and we are all "pregnant," expecting change, awaiting new life, hoping for God to come close to us again. I could feel it in the air. There was a sense of expansion and joy. In Advent it is very appropriate for the whole church to feel pregnant.

And who is the child being born? For whom do we wait? The obvious answer, of course, is Christ. We await the Anointed One, the long-expected Messiah. But perhaps Meister Eckhart, a fourteenth-century monk, pushes us closer to the truth when he states: "What good is it to me if Mary gave birth to the Son of God [1,300] years ago and I don't give birth to God's Son in my person and my culture and my times?"[2] The birth we await involves our own very lives, our own beings.

John the baptizer's words cut to the heart of it: "Repent and receive the baptism for the forgiveness of sins."[3] In other words, get ready for change. Take a new direction. Prepare for personal sacrifice and new responsibilities. Consider the future as open and new. Know that God is coaxing you: "The time is right. You're ready! Relax." Every Christmas our dreams just might come true, for God is coming to be among all people.

Preparing for birth is an exciting yet terrifying time. It is both disorienting and liberating. A part of us will surely die in the process. Gone are the old habits and thought patterns; gone is our need to stay in control and plan everything about the future. Advent is an invitation to be lifted up and turned around to face the One whose name is love. Advent is a time to get ready for our own new birth.

Advent Shock

Florence was such a sturdy woman—stalwart in her faith and in her commitment to the church. She was the mainstay in our kitchen. She cooked for the food festivals and watched over the summer staff as they came and went from our church. She was suspicious of those who cooked for the homeless because she detected equipment slowly disappearing from our kitchen. She prepared the bread and cup for our communion services and offered words of advice as an elder on the church's official board. She was a creative woman who crocheted items to be sold at church bazaars and always hand-made a new baby layette for each child born into the church. Florence was a matriarch of the church.

She had been in fairly good health, until one September day she had a heart attack. It was not a major one, for Florence had gotten up that Sunday morning and had come to church on public transportation. But it was a heart attack all the same. A doctor ordered her into the hospital for tests. For the next two months she was under doctor's orders. Florence was a good patient, undergoing all the tests that had been prescribed for her. Finally the doctors decided that Florence needed heart surgery.

It was so unexpected for Florence to find out that she needed a heart operation. Even though the doctors seemed confident, she wasn't so sure how the surgery would turn out. At first she had refused, saying she was too old for this kind of operation. But the doctors told her of others who had come through with great success. And so, once she had decided to go ahead with it, she was very hopeful.

I have never seen anyone so happy before surgery. She was full of optimism, so excited about the new life that awaited her on the other side of the operation. Florence was able to say both "I'm not afraid to die" and "I want to live." The day before the surgery her whole family came to visit her, even her grandson, whom she hadn't seen in years. I spoke to her on the telephone that day, and she told me confidently, "I'm ready for whatever comes!"

Florence did not regain consciousness following her surgery. Complications had set in; she died two days later. It was a shock to her family and to our whole church to hear this news on the first Sunday in Advent.

During Advent we are waiting for the baby to be born. We are not prepared for the suddenness of death. And yet the Advent texts jolt us out of the here and now and into the end of time. They telescope us to the day of Jesus Christ. Luke says, "People will faint from fear and foreboding of what is coming upon the world, for the powers of the heavens will be shaken."[4] Mark warns, "Beware, keep alert; for you do not know when the time will come."[5] Matthew makes it even more concrete, saying, "Then two will be in the field; one will be taken and one will be left."[6]

How surprising to learn that Advent is not only about birth, but also about death! Advent is about the disintegration of the old order so that the new, true reign of God might come.

Even though it seems strangely out of sync with the season, there is something to be said for preparing for the big day—the day we will meet our Maker. Not one of us knows the hour, so during Advent we are advised to live each day as if it were our last, not in fear or panic, but in joyful celebration and anticipation, "for salvation is nearer to us now than when we first believed."[7]

Crisis, confusion, upheaval . . . advent prepares us. Advent alerts us to our future with God. Advent shakes us out of our complacency. I feel much hope in knowing that Florence was ready to claim her baptismal heritage as a daughter of God's own redeeming on this side of eternity, as well as beyond. On the first Sunday in Advent, then, we raise our heads to glimpse the glory that awaits us in heaven and pray for the strength to stand until that last day.

CHRISTMAS

24-Hour Availability

One year the animals for the Christmas creche arrived in the middle of a rainstorm—a great big northeaster. The wind was so strong that it blew down the steeple at St. Augustine's Church a block away. Part of the structure had fallen onto the Benjamin Franklin Bridge, closing it to traffic. Many members of our congregation had called the church office that morning to see how we were doing. Some even reported that their coworkers had been concerned when they heard about a church steeple falling in Old City. "Your church is in Old City. Maybe it's your church," they suggested. "Don't worry," Elizabeth, our board president, replied calmly. "Our church doesn't *have* a steeple!"

The men were nearly two hours late with the trailer carrying the animals. The mishap at St. Augustine's forced them to make a detour across the Walt Whitman Bridge, south of the city, then find their way to the church through an unfamiliar maze of city streets. When they finally arrived, they backed their trailer right up to the fence, opened the rear gate, and led the animals out, into the creche. The sheep and goats went willingly, but the cow and donkey had to be pushed. The whole procedure took less than five minutes. It happened so matter-of-factly. In previous years, traffic usually stopped, and each of the animals was carried out or led out with a rope. This time the delivery was quick and easy. And there were no cameras: the media were focused on St. Augustine's shattered steeple up the street. The rain kept falling quite steadily, and the wind kept blowing. No pedestrians came by to welcome the animals. Even the animals were unusually quiet, preferring the indoor stable, where it was still dry.

After the storm cleared, people began to telephone, inquiring when they might come to see the animals. They wanted to make an appointment, if they could. They wanted to make sure the animals would be available when they arrived. How surprised people are when they learn they can come anytime, day or night! There is no fee, no waiting line, no time schedule. No appointment is needed. The animals are simply here, present, available. The creche is open twenty-four hours a day!

For some this news is a surprise. For others it is an offense: "How dare you keep the animals up all night. It's too cold! Why don't you take them inside? They'll get sick. What if something happens?" We seem so disconnected from nature that we don't realize most farm animals have no trouble withstanding the cold of the outdoors. Maybe, being sophisticated urbanites, we mistrust the city environment as a place of safety for any living being.

But the offense can also develop into a scandal. There is *no* closing time, *no* admission requirements, *no* age limit? Anyone can come? You can spend as long as you want? You can come back everyday, or several times a day, no matter what the weather is like?

In a time when most public attractions are becoming privatized, our Christmas creche is totally accessible to everybody, every day of the week, all hours of the day and night. Total accessibility. How risky, how outrageously vulnerable our Christmas creche is! It's so unassuming, so simple.

And that's the way it is with God. God is simply with us, totally available, one hundred percent of the time. We'd like to sign up, stand in line, make an appointment, present our credentials—isn't that what you do for someone really important? Maybe we could fax our list of references. We want time to prepare properly to make our way into God's good graces. All this availability is frightening! In the face of everything we think we have, God seems to be nothing. It's not until we realize how little we actually have that we stand ready to receive all that God is.

God is so much a part of our lives, so utterly at home in the universe, so undeniably close, so completely involved with all that is alive, that we run the risk of missing God altogether. Here is the real scandal; here is the danger: that even at Christmas time, we'll be so distracted by all our activities that we'll miss God's presence in the simple and ordinary ways God comes to us.

Anthony de Mello, the late Jesuit and spiritual teacher from India, describes a dialogue between a seeker and a spiritually wise master:

> *"Where shall I look for Enlightenment?"*
> *"Here."*
> *"When will it happen?"*
> *"It is happening right now."*
> *"Then why don't I experience it?"*
> *"Because you do not look."*
> *"What should I look for?"*
> *"Nothing. Just look."*

"At what?"
"Anything your eyes alight upon."
"Must I look in a special kind of way?"
"No. The ordinary way will do."
"But don't I always look the ordinary way?"
"No."
"Whyever not?"
"Because to look you must be here. You're mostly somewhere else."[8]

How can we live in the here and now long enough to really see? How can *we* be simply available to God, as God is simply available to us, twenty-four hours a day? God's love seeks our attentiveness, our patience, our faithful response. Is this also part of the Christmas story?

Getting Our Goats

One year the animals arrived on Friday the thirteenth. And what a surprise the farmer had in store for us. Instead of sheep, he sent us goats! Yes, two frisky miniature kids!

At first I was disappointed. Goats! Goats in the Christmas creche? Where are the sheep? How can we have shepherds if we don't have any sheep? We love those woolly little creatures. How can we celebrate Christmas without them?

But I began to see value in the goats, especially those cute little kids. They were able to climb everywhere, even on the roof of the stable. This feat used to frighten me. I was afraid the kids would jump out of the creche. Then I saw another one of their tricks. To the delight of the spectators, especially the children, these little kids began to show off by walking—sometimes it even appeared they were dancing—on the back of the cow. It seemed like our Christmas creche was deteriorating into a three-ring circus.

Another year we had a couple of goats mixed in with the sheep. In comparison with the lively miniature kids, the larger goats were a bit disappointing. They acted quite shy and stayed in the rear of the stable. They appeared rather sheepish to me, and I began to wonder if they were really sheep, dressed in goat's clothing!

One never could tell what the goats were going to do next.

They loved to knock down the mannequins, strewing their clothes all around the stable. Early one Christmas morning the goats had been at it again. When I came out to look at the creche, everything was in disarray. Some of the shepherds even had their heads knocked off. Clothes were everywhere! Joseph had fallen over backwards and was leaning against the side of the stable, and Mary had tipped forward into the hay. It looked like the whole bunch of characters had been up all night partying.

A woman came by with her children, and I commented, "Isn't this how many of us feel on Christmas morning?" In an odd way, it seemed somehow appropriate, considering what had happened to Mary, Joseph, and the shepherds the night before.

Goats—goats in the nativity scene. They bring delight and a touch of reality to it all. I wouldn't want my church members to hear this, but even in the church, it makes for much more fun to have a few goats mixed in with the sheep!

The Cow's Mournful Cry

The cow cried. All night long she moaned. Yes, one year the cow in our outdoor Christmas creche had a difficult time adjusting to life in the big city.

I felt sorry for her. I suffered with her. On her first day at Fourth and Race Streets, she cried all night. Her mournful moan reverberated off the buildings around the church, amplifying the sound so that it seemed to be coming from all directions. I lay awake trying to figure out what to do. This was only the first night of the animals' stay at our outdoor Christmas creche, and I did not know how I was going to get through the next two weeks.

I began to think of my neighbors in nearby apartment buildings. Were they lying awake too? Funny, isn't it? I hear police sirens all the time, and even the louder noise of fire trucks as they rush by on an emergency run, and I sleep on. But the cry of this cow kept me awake all night.

There were a few times, though, when she stopped crying, and then I began to worry all the more. What's happening now? You see, the cow had me hooked. I was concerned about her. I watched her every move, and when I walked by the stable, I waved to her. So did other people. That cry was definitely part of her strategy. She lured people in with her mournful moo.

And when you wanted to leave her side by the fence, she would let out another sorrowful sound.

One man spent a long time with her—much longer than he had intended. He kept looking at his watch every few minutes. He had somewhere else to go. Several times he tried to break away, but she kept him there. When he finally headed for his car in the parking lot across the street, the cow cried. The man turned around and shrugged his shoulders in disbelief.

When people left her side, the cow turned to the mannequins representing Mary, Joseph, the shepherds, and the Magi. Imagine, she tried to wake up these lifeless statues! She poked and nudged, trying to make them come alive. She persisted until they fell over and lost their headpieces and scarves.

What a cow she was! What a presence she had in the Christmas creche! In fact, she more than made up for the lack of sheep in that year's nativity scene. We won't forget her and her attempt to bring us in for a closer look and a chance to get acquainted. This cow obviously needed people.

There would have been a time when an acquaintance with a cow would not have been such a strange and troubling experience. In the past, farm animals lived close to people. Barns were attached to farmhouses, and in cold weather, people slept next to the animals just to keep warm.

In the city we have such little contact with the natural world of animals and birds and fish. We look at them from a distance and worry about their catching cold when the wind blows. Many people call to tell me how uncomfortable the animals must be. They feel we mistreat them by keeping them outdoors day and night. But I reassure these people that the animals are well cared for. They can go inside the stable at night, when it rains, or when they want protection from the cold wind. On the farm they spend most of the time outdoors. Did you know that a cow is not in danger until the thermometer drops to thirty degrees below zero?

But why focus on the cow? How does she fit into the Christmas story? We don't really know if a cow was present at the birth, although three times in his second chapter, Luke, the author of the nativity story in the Bible, mentions that Mary wrapped the babe in swaddling clothes and *laid him in a manger.* So we know from Luke's mention of the manger that some animals must have been present at the birth. It's remarkable—Christ was born in the midst of the animal world as well as the human one.

Kenneth Grahame, in his children's classic *The Wind in the Willows,* writes:

> And then they heard the angels tell
> "Who were the first to cry Nowell?
> Animals all, as it befell,
> In the stable where they did dwell!
> Joy shall be theirs in the morning!"[9]

The poet J. Barrie Shepherd calls the animals "The Silent Seers" when he writes:

> Of all the witnesses
> around that holy manger
> perhaps it was the animals
> saw best what lay ahead
> for they had paced the aching roads

slept in the wet and hungry fields
known the sharp sting of sticks
and thorns and curses
endured the constant bruise
of burdens not their own
the tendency of men to use
and then discard rather than meet
and pay the debt of gratitude.
For them the future also held
the knacker's rope, the flayer's blade
the tearing of their bodies
for the sparing of a race.
In the shadows of that stable
might it be his warmest welcome
lay within their quiet comprehending gaze?[10]

In the incarnation, God comes very close. "Here is the Lamb of God who takes away the sin of the world!"[11] In the incarnation God comes to redeem not just humankind, but the whole created order. God comes to call us back to one another and to what it means to be a human being, integrated into all of creation. In the incarnation, Jesus comes among us to help us learn how to live in this wilderness, as the animals do, and to make it all sacred, holy.

The message of Christmas is an earthy one. It addresses our deepest loneliness, our clearest alienation from one another, from ourselves, from the created order, and from the Creator. Christmas gives us a new creation story, one we share with the animals and the natural world. Christ's birth in the midst of animals restores new integrity to the whole of creation. The cow's mournful cry on a cold night is a powerful symbol that awakens us humans to our common fate with all of creation, as Jesus comes to close the gap between God and all of God's creation.

Joseph's Turn

At Christmas we usually hear about Mary, the shepherds, the angels, the Magi, and even the star. Rarely do we think of Joseph. He usually stands at the back of the Christmas stable, almost hidden from view. But—Mary, shepherds, Magi, move over. It's Joseph's turn!

One year we had a very interesting Joseph. Barry, the father of the twins who were to be baby Jesus on Christmas Eve, was to play the role of Joseph. That's right—we were to have twins in our Christmas creche. One was Jesus at the outdoor manger; the other was Jesus at the indoor service. And their father, Barry, is a real carpenter. He works for a construction firm that builds schools and hospitals—big projects—all over the region. In 1983 when the Reverend H. Daehler Hayes, the first Christmas creche builder, resigned as pastor of Old First to become Minister of the Rhode Island Conference of the United Church of Christ, Barry took over the job as chief carpenter of the Christmas stable. He is certainly well qualified for the task and handles it with great skill.

One year, however, Barry couldn't come out for construction day because of unexpected work. Maybe this was fortuitous, because this time I wanted Barry to play a different role. My hope was that Barry would be center stage, portraying Joseph on Christmas Eve. I said *my hope* was that Barry would be Joseph. You see, Barry is a very modest fellow. He's not very happy taking such an up-front role. He doesn't like to call attention to himself.

Just before Thanksgiving I visited Barry to ask him very officially, "How 'bout it? We've got to have a Joseph to walk with Mary and the baby in the pageant on Christmas Eve. Are you able to come? Would you be willing to be Joseph this year?"

"I don't know," Barry hesitated. "I'll have to think about it." That was the best response I could get.

And so it was with the real Joseph. He too was reluctant to take the part. Matthew writes that when Mary was "found to be with child from the Holy Spirit,"[12] Joseph "planned to dismiss her quietly."[13] He didn't want to become involved in this unplanned pregnancy, this unexpected turn of events. He didn't want to disgrace Mary publicly, but he also didn't want his name associated with her news. He wanted to play it safe, back out of it graciously, remain anonymously in the background.

But there were those darned dreams. They kept recurring, and there was this voice: "Do not be afraid to take Mary as your wife, for the child conceived in her is from the Holy Spirit."[14] The voice urged him on.

Joseph's role is essential. He has to name the baby, to take legal responsibility in the eyes of society. Through Joseph, Jesus is linked to the House of David and becomes an offspring of the root of Jesse. Through Joseph, Jesus is given not just a legal name, but a specific identity among a people with whom God has a special relationship.

Joseph's role should not be relegated to the back of the creche. Though he was reluctant at first, in the end Joseph listened to his dreams and became the one who not only named

Jesus but saved him from Herod's army by taking Mary and the baby and escaping to Egypt. Through Joseph, "Jesus, the one who saves" was saved for the salvation of the whole world.

Ann Weems includes a poem about Joseph in her book of Christmas poetry, *Kneeling in Bethlehem:*

> Who put Joseph in the back of the stable?
> Who dressed him in brown, put a staff in his hand,
>   and told him to stand in the back of the creche,
>   background for the magnificent light of the
>   Madonna?
>
> God–chosen, this man Joseph was faithful
>   in spite of the gossip in Nazareth,
>   in spite of the danger from Herod.
> This man, Joseph, listened to angels
>   and it was he who named the child Emmanuel.
> Is this a man to be stuck for centuries
>   in the back of the stable?[15]

Barry did make it on Christmas Eve to play the part of Joseph. He overcame his hesitancy and stood by the manger. We can't have the Christmas story without him. Someone will have to come forward to play the part of Joseph.

All of us sooner or later have to come forward. We have to make it through our reluctance and our fears. We have to take on roles we haven't chosen. Sometimes there is no choice; circumstances demand that we get involved.

Recently I came across a news photo I clipped several years ago and filed away. I saved the clipping because it reminded me of a male version of the traditional Madonna-and-child pose. It showed Arbab Mohamed holding his son in his arms in the Derubed drought camp in Ethiopia. Mohamed's wife had died of starvation, and Mohamed had to take care of their child.

Today there are countless Mohameds, modern-day Josephs, who have come out of anonymity to care for children, some children who are their own and some who have been given to them by circumstance. Unfortunately, parents continue to die. Someone has to see that the children are fed. Some relatives may be doing it unwillingly, but they push through their own reluctance to do their part.

Christmas is about this kind of risk-taking, this kind of reaching out, this kind of involvement. When God needs us we have to break through our insecurities and perplexities to be of help. At Christmas we recognize all who have the courage to participate in saving the children, as we honor Joseph, who did it with such grace and faithfulness.

Baptized for the Manger

In the years since I have been collecting stories about our live-animal Christmas creche, people have come to me to share some of their observations. Michael's mother, for example, told me a story that had happened some years ago. A friend who was a photographer had been visiting her. He wanted to take some unusual photos of Philadelphia scenes, not the typical tourist shots of Independence Hall and the Liberty Bell. "I've got the place for you!" she volunteered.

At midnight she brought her visitor to our Christmas creche. Lots of people were gathered around, pointing and laughing. There was havoc in the manger. The baby Jesus had been tossed aside, and a young calf had climbed in. Happily the photographer had found the unique photo opportunity he had been looking for!

Baptized for the manger! Recently I have been thinking about what a daring venture it is to place one of our own children in the Christmas Eve manger. But in many ways that is what happens to *all* the children who are baptized in the church. In baptism, each child takes on the identity of Christ, and so each must go to the manger.

I was very touched by the comment of one mother whose child was to play the role of Jesus on Christmas Eve. She said, "I think we better baptize Jane *before* Christmas Eve, *before* she goes into the manger." How right she was! Baptism initiates a new identity in Christ as the child takes the name Christian and the parents promise to grow with the child in the Christian faith. Jane began her Christian career quite early as she assumed the central role in our Christmas Eve tableau that year.

When we take our children right from the baptismal font to the manger we are saying, "You are special. We need you to participate in our common life." My hope is that we continue to say that to children of all ages, for they are so much a part of our ministry.

Scripture offers few details of Jesus' formative years, of his growth from infancy into adulthood. There is the story of his visit to the Temple in Jerusalem at the age of twelve, and then nothing until he begins his public ministry eighteen years later. But it's not difficult to imagine what Jesus was like during his growing-up years. We get to experience it right in our own congregation as all the little ones who've played Jesus in the creche on Christmas Eve grow up right before our very eyes. Jane and Steven, Julius and Jonathan, Dana and Craig . . . , the list goes on and on. We see them grow, week in and week out. We see them change and yet somehow remain the same.

The elderly, homebound members of the congregation frequently ask me about the children. Dorothy, a long-time member of the church who now lives in a retirement home some distance away, remembered several of the little ones from when she was a regular attendee. "The Stutzman's grandson, born to an Armenian father—what's his name? He was born on my birthday. I remember, he was such a bundle of energy. And Kevin, Florence's great-grandchild, whatever happened to him?" I explained that Kevin is an acolyte now. "Oh," Dorothy remarked, "that would have meant so much to Florence." It was remarkable to see how important our children were to Dorothy.

This is one of the marvelous aspects of the church: we have this family connection. We belong to one another because we belong to Christ. Our baptism initiates us into a big family where, in the tension of growing up, we learn what it means to be a human being as we all take on the identity of Christ.

Welcoming an Unknown Child

One day I went to Collingdale to visit Mary and Joseph. Yes, Mary and Joseph live in Collingdale, a southwest suburb of Philadelphia, on a small street just off MacDade Boulevard.

I first heard about Mary and Joseph from Mary's mother, who is a long-time member of our church. Though not active members today, Mary and Joseph met and married years ago when both were young people in our congregation. I was eager to get acquainted with them because I had heard so much about them from others.

When I arrived Mary was home alone. Joseph was working. He is a driver–sales representative for St. Mary's Laundry in Philadelphia and has a regular route on the Main Line, a wealthy suburban stretch of small towns west of the city. But I really shouldn't say that Mary was alone. In the house under her care were six children—four infants and two toddlers.

As I entered the small duplex, I found Mary busy with the children. Three of them were napping—one in a playpen, two in cribs. A fourth child, however, was very much awake in a small seat on the floor. The living-dining room was filled with things of children—toys, diapers, a bassinet, two cribs, and the playpen.

Mary and Joseph are foster parents. They have been foster parents for thirty years, and in their simple home in Collingdale have helped to raise, along with three children of their own, more than a hundred children of all ages, races, and backgrounds.

Mary told me about the children currently in her care. "Three of them are crack babies," she commented. "More and more of our babies are addicted. They were addicted to drugs at birth because their mothers were on drugs during their pregnancies." One of the babies had been treated for syphilis at birth, in addition to the drug addiction. Another came to them at three months of age because her home had no heat, no beds, no blankets, no food. A third child, the one who was wide awake during my visit, was placed with this foster family at four months, when she weighed only six pounds. She was just days from death because of failure to thrive. Now, two-and-a-half months later, this baby weighs fourteen pounds.

Last of all I met Tamika, who will be the baby Jesus in our live Christmas creche on Christmas Eve. The youngest of the babies, she slept soundly through my visit. Tamika has three siblings, two of them with emotional disabilities and living in foster homes. Her oldest sister, at age fifteen, has AIDS. She has run away from every foster home where she has been placed and is so emotionally injured that she lives on the street. So Tamika came immediately to foster care when she was only nine days old.

What special children they are, I thought, and how amazing are the love and care that Joseph and Mary give them! Two of the children have to wear heart monitors. Mary now sleeps on the living room sofa so she can hear the monitors during the night and record the information.

With some of the children so sickly, Mary admitted that she spends much time at various clinics where the children are treated at no charge. "But you must wait your turn. It's endless," Mary added. Because she doesn't drive, she has to get a sitter for the other children and take public transportation to medical appointments. "It has its moments," confided Mary, "but it's a life we love. The language of children is easy to understand. It doesn't take much to meet their needs. Some people, when they hear about us, think that our home must be a madhouse, but it's really quite peaceful." And so it was the day I visited.

I was deeply touched by this special "holy" couple. They are connected to the suffering, hurting world on a daily basis through the children they have accepted into their home. Hunger, drugs, sexual abuse, emotional deprivation are all familiar to them. "We are supposed to treat every crack baby as if he or she has AIDS. Some people won't take these children, but I'm not afraid. We have to take a few extra precautions, that's all," Mary reflected.

Happily, Mary and Joseph prepare most of their foster children for adoption or to be returned to their natural parents. "All have gone willingly," Mary told me. "If I have enough advance warning, we can prepare them beautifully for the transition."

What a holy, loving, caring family this is. Mary, no longer a teenager, stands in the long tradition of special older women, like Sarah and Hannah, to whom God has promised a new family. Joseph, being a bit older as well, resembles the New Testament figure who is open to trusting a strange story and able to accept and take responsibility for children who are not his own. And our Jesus—tiny Tamika, so weak, vulnerable, and threatened by death at an early age—faces an uncertain future, wrought with difficulties, just as Jesus did.

This Holy Family, these three special people, announce that Christmas didn't happen just two thousand years ago. It is not a long ago, ancient, romanticized story. Christmas is here and now. Mary and Joseph and the baby are contemporary. And the miracle of God's love continues to reach out to us through them. This is what it means to welcome an unknown child.

That Unquenchable Spirit

*

They're back! Friday morning promptly at ten o'clock the animals arrived for our live-animal Christmas creche. And starting then, people have been here to see them. The *Daily News* has already reported on their arrival with a photo and article titled "Old City's Sheepish Inn Is Yuletide Tradition."

The sheep are wonderful. We have three of them. They are still the shy ones in the creche, frequently hiding in the back of the stable. But there's a goat that has no problem being out front. And of course we have a donkey and a cow to round out the nativity scene.

There's so much to learn from the Christmas creche. The animals seem to have personalities of their own, and it's interesting to watch how they struggle to get along in the confines of the stable and the courtyard.

One year, when the month of December was one of the coldest in Philadelphia's history, many people worried about the animals and kept calling the church office, begging us to do something, anything, to keep the animals warm. When I telephoned the farmer to convey all the worried messages I had received, he was confident. He assured me that the animals were used to this kind of weather and would survive it well.

One night after eleven o'clock a young couple knocked on my door and really insisted that we bring the animals inside the church building for the night. I told them I couldn't do that because inside the church social hall we had twenty men without a place to stay. The men, I argued, would surely freeze on the street. But the animals will be all right. "OK," they said, "it's on *your* conscience." Wow!

A few evenings later, right in the midst of that cold spell, Marge came running up the stairs to my room. "Geneva," she cried, her voice trembling, "you won't believe what's happening out at the creche." Her face looked terrified. "The cow's giving birth," she shouted. "It's all happening right out in the stable."

Immediately I put on my coat and ran out. Janet was there, and she too was crying. What an anxious moment! The cow wouldn't let us get close enough to see what was really happening. She was very protective of the calf. But we could definitely see another body there in the straw.

Once again I telephoned the farmer.

This time he was surprised—and then he laughed. "Well, she really fooled me this time!"

"Don't worry," he insisted. "The mother knows what to do. Everything will be all right. I'll drive by in the morning."

"But it's cold," I replied, "and the calf's not moving. We think something might be wrong." I wanted to have a vet come over to check out everything.

"No," the farmer reassured me. "There's nothing you need to do. Last week I had a cow give birth on the open field, and everything was fine," he said with certitude.

"Well, okay," I thought. It sounded convincing to me. There's nothing to do. Nature will take care of itself. What an urbanized person I've become! I have no choice but to rely on the advice of the farmer.

I was so stirred by the event that I called a few church members just to let them know what was happening. A real birth in the manger—imagine! Should I call the newspapers? They might like to get a scoop on the story.

But the next morning the calf was gone.

Later the farmer telephoned, and I learned that the newborn calf had died. I was upset. What could this mean? It's difficult to deal with death in the creche. We expect to find life there. Death in the creche is jolting—unsettling.

The shock was personal, as well. During the year I had been dealing with a heavy dose of death: not only the death of a friend and of beloved church members, but also the death of a church project that seemed essential to the growth of our urban congregation and its ministry. The church's historic schoolhouse, located just south of our church building, had been erected in 1791 by the congregation as a parochial school. The building, not available when the church returned to its original location in the late 1960s, was now for sale. The church had been trying to acquire it for more than twenty years, and, just when the transaction was about to become reality, the deal fell through. The project died. The schoolhouse was sold to someone else, and we did not have the chance to give birth to this possibility to expand our facilities for mission in the city. Once again, the Christmas creche mirrored life. It reflected what we had been going through as a congregation.

I couldn't talk about this incident of death in the creche for quite a long while. I wanted the calf to live. Wouldn't that have been a good story? But the calf had died, and I couldn't face it. It all was so sad.

After Christmas I went to Florida to attend a national

United Church of Christ pastors' conference. The theme of the gathering was "The Pastor as Preacher," and we heard several sermons a day by some of the best preachers in the country.

One of them was the Reverend Peter Gomes, chaplain at Harvard University. The subject of his sermon was hope. He gave a very scholarly sermon on hope as the enduring enterprise of the gospel. Mr. Gomes went through a whole scriptural text, verse by verse, underlining the hope that is at the heart of the New Testament.

When he finished, there were questions. "What do you do," one person asked, "when hope dies? Can you still preach about hope? Can you take people beyond the hopelessness they feel?"

Other questions were posed, and then an African American pastor from San Diego, the Reverend James Hargett, rose to speak. He said, "We of the African American tradition can always go beyond hope. We have to—all the time. There's a line in the Negro National Anthem," he continued, "which states that 'hope, unborn, has died.' But," he added, "we go on—we go on, because we believe in the ongoing fertility of the womb. We go on because we believe that the womb is still capable of producing new life."

What a help these comments were to me! Disappointment, discouragement, failure, and defeat can stop us in our tracks. We want to give up. We find it difficult to keep on hoping. Death can paralyze us. Defeat can kill our confidence. But the womb is still fertile—life is still filled with the possibilities of new birth. We can go beyond discouragement and even death when we realize that the womb is still capable of producing new life.

Now the animals have returned. The Christmas creche is

full of life again. We probably have another pregnant cow. It finally dawned on me: each year we've never needed to milk the cow. She's been dry because she's been pregnant.

There is something about the spirit of Christmas that is undefeatable. Every year we are introduced to its unquenchable spirit. Every year Christmas revives the latent hope that is within us and reminds us that life can keep on giving, and defeat and despair do not have to have the last word.

Twins in the Manger

Twins! Twins in the manger! Can you imagine that? It's not part of the traditional Christmas story, but that's what we had one Christmas Eve.

Each year God has faithfully given us a baby for our Christmas manger. If we have a boy, then Christ is a boy. If we have a girl, Christ is a girl. If we have an African American child, then Christ is African American—or German American or Hispanic. This year God has been especially generous and has given us twins!

The doctor's announcement that there would be two babies caused quite a stir in Barry and Jeanne's household. They already had one daughter, Carrie, now age five. Another child would have been great—but two! Barry and Jeanne weren't sure they could handle two babies at the same time.

In August the twins were born, and they're both doing very well. Their parents are adjusting, and it's been a special joy to have the grandparents of the babies in the congregation too! It's a privilege to see the thrill and delight of two generations as they marvel at what God has done.

Both babies were with us on Christmas Eve. Together they are a sign of God's extraordinary generosity. It wouldn't have been fair to select only one of them to be Jesus; so Jenna was baby Jesus outdoors at the 6:30 P.M. service, and Jessica was Jesus indoors at the 7:30 P.M. candlelight service. Few people noticed that the babies were different because they're identical.

As I thought about these twins, I remembered the Old Testament twins, Jacob and Esau, whose story is recorded in the Book of Genesis. They were not identical twins. In fact, they were as different as day and night. They fought each other and struggled over who was to receive their father's blessing and the family inheritance. As twin stories go, it's not a pleasant one. The story is filled with struggle and deceit, animosity and rivalry.

I tried to imagine what twins in our manger would be like. Would they get along with each other, or would they be rivals? If Jesus had had a twin, would the ill will we see in Jacob and Esau be theirs as well? Somehow it seems in keeping with the Prince-of-Peace tradition to have two babies in the manger who would be able to get along and show the whole world what true reconciliation is all about.

How might such an apocryphal story develop? I tried to envision the visit of the Magi and the flight into Egypt—with twins. Perhaps Mary and Joseph might have decided to leave one of the babies in Egypt with the family who had welcomed them, in order to ensure the survival of at least one child during the slaughter of the innocent children. I can even imagine an ending to the story: the twins reunited, years later, as Jesus is headed to Jerusalem to face the cross.

In the midst of my Advent musings about twins, a visiting German New Testament theologian arrived to spend a few days at my home. When I told him about my speculation over twins in the manger, he said, "That's not such a farfetched idea." Then he told me about the twin tradition in the early church, as recorded in the Gospel of Thomas. According to this non-canonical Gnostic text, the disciple Thomas, whose name means "twin," taught that people who become followers of Jesus take on a new identity. Through baptism, they become part of a new community in which, as they share the characteristics of Christ, they become Jesus' own brothers and sisters.

Later, as recorded in the Gnostic writing Acts of Thomas, we learn that the disciple Thomas traveled to India, where he preached and taught, healed the sick, and performed miracles, just as Jesus had done. Sometimes people mistook this disciple, this twin, for Jesus, saying, "He has the same face, the same expression . . . he looks just like Jesus."[16]

In this way we can begin to understand the words of the apostle Paul who wrote during this same formative period of the early church: "I have been crucified with Christ; and it is no longer I who live, but it is Christ who lives in me. And the life I now live in the flesh I live by faith in the Son of God, who loved me and gave himself for me."[17]

So, having twins in the manger is not the foolish idea I had at first imagined. We become Jesus' twin as we live the life he taught. Like Paul and Thomas, we put on Christ when we are baptized. The purpose of the Christian life is to be transformed, so that we may be conformed to the image and likeness of God's own Child. God became one of us, so we might become like God—and find our way back to God. Christ is the firstborn within a large family, in which we also have part.

Twins—twins in the manger—twins in our Christmas creche! While one twin is up front, visible for all to see, the other twin is hidden in the congregation, among the great body of believers. Perhaps we who come to the creche on Christmas Eve, the most holy of nights, come to rediscover and reclaim our own true identity as twins of Jesus.

Christmas Eve Brawl

The holidays are always difficult for the men who stay in our church's shelter for the homeless. They remember years past when things were better for them. Tensions build up over very little matters, and fights can break out easily.

Usually we try to make Christmas Eve as homelike as possible at the shelter. Typically there's a festive meal prepared by volunteers, special Christmas music, and gifts for everyone. I am always amazed at all that is showered upon the men during the holiday season. Sometimes it's even embarrassing. A warm hat, two pairs of gloves, thermal underwear, sweatshirts, warm socks, cologne, toiletries, candy, fruit, nuts. Where will these men, who have no permanent place to sleep, store it all? The poor among us may be more aware of the glut of the holiday season than many of us are.

On this particular Christmas Eve, a heavy rain was coming down outside. It was not a pleasant evening. We had had our outdoor Christmas tableau in the midst of the rainstorm, but the event had been shortened considerably. The crowd was not as large as usual because of the wet weather. Many people had chosen to stay home. For the men of the shelter, it was indeed a blessing to have a roof over their heads, to be dry and indoors. But tensions were in the air inside the shelter too. Was it the uneasiness of holiday memories, or the drenching winter weather?

After the meal there was a short time to relax and mingle with volunteers before gifts were distributed. Suddenly we heard a loud noise, followed by shouting. A fight was in full swing. The supervisor stepped in to break up the fight and calm the situation. When the violence had abated, and there was a moment of calm, the supervisor asked both men to leave. That is the rule: when there is a fight, both men have to leave for thirty days. There is never an attempt to decide who is right and who is wrong. Both must leave on the spot. They cannot even stay the night. The premise behind this rule is that it takes two to fight. Both are wrong to be involved in the fight, so both must leave. It's a hard punishment, especially on this wet and holy night. But a goal of the shelter is peace, tranquillity, no fighting. Let there be peace in the shelter and on earth goodwill to all.

But one of the men didn't want to leave. It was Christmas Eve and very wet outside. He had nowhere to go. He begged to stay and even began to cry. The shelter supervisor tried to quiet him and politely reminded him that he had to leave. But this man, determined not to be put out, kept up his protest all the more. How unfair it seemed to be kicked out onto the street on Christmas Eve! It's a night when there should be room in the inn for everyone, even those who fight. Finally the supervisor called the police.

The police had no reason to take the man to jail, yet he begged them to do so. Jail would be a better place to spend Christmas Eve than out in the pouring rain. But the police were adamant—he had done nothing to land him in jail. So filled with anger at the unpleasant circumstances of his holiday, the man took a wild punch at the side of the wooden stairway leading up to our church sanctuary. The boards creaked as if to relieve their pain, and the man's hand stung too! So now he demanded that the police officers take him to the hospital to have his hand X-rayed.

And that's what happened. The man spent the whole night, all of Christmas Eve, at the local hospital. It was so much better than being out in the wet weather. What persistence, what faith! The man, like the importune woman before the unjust judge in Luke's Gospel, demanded God's hospitality in his life. Ironically on that cold, damp, holy night, the hospital, rather than the church, became a place of hospitality for a wounded, hurting child of God.

God's Gift of Reconciliation

On Christmas Eve, Old First has an outdoor service at the manger and a beautiful indoor candlelight service. But on Christmas morning, there are more people from the community in our church sanctuary than church members. Half the congregants on Christmas Day have spent Christmas Eve on the street or in shelters; the others are friends of the homeless or people who work with them. We gather together to receive some bread and wine, gifts of God's love poured out on us all.

The homeless usher all of us into the spirit of the day. The holidays are quite difficult for them. They struggle with bad memories from past Christmases and take nothing for granted. I remember one year that we delayed the start of the service because one man was at the communion table just gazing and gazing at the Christchild placed in the center. The homeless approach the communion table simply—uncertain, helpless, grieving, empty, waiting. They come as they are, poor and needy, vulnerable and frail . . . and then the gift is given—to all of us!

I'll never forget how it happened one Christmas Day, right there in our church sanctuary. It began during the prayers of intercession as homeless and formerly homeless people prayed for circumstances and people close to them. It continued during the singing of "I Wonder As I Wander" by Priscilla, who walked among us dressed as a bag lady. And God's very special presence stayed with us through the eucharist as we came together to eat around the same table. Tears welled up in many eyes as we realized in a profoundly new way how deeply we are all connected to one another. We are brothers and sisters, related to one another because we belong to God. Reconciliation came quickly as we were given the same wonderful gift of Christmas—God's renewing and redeeming love. It was a marvelous moment that lasted almost twenty minutes. That's a long time to be truly united in God's presence, fully aware of who we all are as God's redeemed people.

The feasting always continues downstairs in the church social hall, where the homeless sit around large tables ready to be served. They look like kings, seated there. And lined up along the kitchen wall, ready to serve them, are the people from the suburbs and the Main Line. In the words of Howard Thurman, the work of Christmas has begun:

> To find the lost,
> To heal the broken,
> To feed the hungry,
> To release the prisoner,
> To rebuild the nations,
> To bring peace among the people,
> To make music in the heart.[18]

Life Keeps on Coming

Old First members sign up to welcome the many visitors who come to see our live-animal creche on Saturday and Sunday afternoons. It's a great way to be involved in the Christmas story, especially for the children. They don't need to hide their enthusiasm. Quite eagerly, children and adults alike invite our visitors to return to worship with us at one of our special holiday services. The Christmas creche is a great place to be an evangelist. The story tells itself!

One Sunday Larry and Lee Ann were greeting at the Christmas creche when they met Gene and Monique. Monique just loved the animals; Gene was looking for a place where he and his "adopted" daughter could attend worship on a regular basis. Of course, Larry extended an invitation to our eleven o'clock Sunday morning services and eagerly announced to me that they would be coming one of these next weeks. It took almost a month, but finally Monique and Gene arrived in February, when we were celebrating Black History Month.

From the moment they entered our doors, Gene and Monique told me, they felt at home. Within a month they decided to join the church. Monique became an acolyte, and Gene began to teach first grade in our church school. We soon learned what a gift Gene has with children.

Every Sunday when Gene stopped by Monique's house to

bring her to church, neighborhood children observed the two of them going out, all dressed up. These children wondered where Gene and Monique were going, looking so stylish. They wanted to know if they could come too. So, slowly, with the permission of their parents, Gene began to bring more children to church with him. He developed a real following. There is Rashida, Quaheem, Michelle, and Kasmeen. When Monique stays with her grandmother in another part of town, Gene has to leave his home at 6 A.M. in order to pick up all the children and be at church by nine—that is, if everyone is ready on time. After church Gene usually takes the children to a play, a concert, or a museum. By four o'clock Gene begins to drop the children back at their homes, so that by six when he gets home, Gene has put in a full day. At nearly seventy years of age, Gene says Sunday evenings he is "exhausted."

But Gene is quick to add, "Maybe I am taking on too hard an endeavor, but the children start calling by Thursday wanting to go to church, and I am their only source. I am glad I can help these young people, and I enjoy doing so."

Gene perceptively comments on what a difference coming to church has made in the lives of these children. He says it happens so naturally. You bring them, and something new opens up in their lives. Now Gene's natural daughter, Barbara, and her husband, Willi, have joined our church. The numbers keep growing. And just think: it all started with Larry and Lee Ann's invitation at the Christmas creche!

A Special Day for Seniors

Many people think Christmas is for children. They think Christmas appeals to the innocence of the young. These folk feel that children come easily to faith, that children readily trust God and believe the story of Christ's coming to be born among us in the stable with the animals.

One year, however, I spent the days before Christmas with the seniors of our widespread congregation. I usually try to visit all the homebound members of our church during Advent, but for some reason I was unable to see many of them early in the season. Seniors are busy people, even those who are homebound. They have all kinds of appointments—with the doctor, the physical therapist, the hairdresser. So it wasn't easy for me to squeeze in a visit.

On my Christmas rounds with these seniors, I decided to ask each of them: "What does Christmas mean to you? What is this special season of the year all about? What do you hope for at Christmas?"

I was astonished by the answers I heard. The first person I queried was Mary, age ninety-three. She is the oldest of a large family and still feels the responsibility for her two younger sisters, Ann and Grace, who live in the same retirement community. When I visited on Monday morning, Mary's two sisters were with her, and Mary promptly opened the Christmas goodies the women of our church had sent. As the good older sister she is, Mary shared the contents of the package with the three of us. We had an impromptu Christmas party as we all enjoyed the cookies and candies.

It was then that I decided to ask my question. "Mary, what does Christmas mean to you?" And immediately Mary had an answer that startled me. "Christmas is about the Lord's coming to earth and suffering on the cross for us—and especially for me, and for each person in particular." I was surprised at this response. I had not expected anyone to make the direct link between Christmas and Easter, but Mary's faith looks backward from Easter to Christmas, the way I think the Christmas story was first envisioned.

At this point, one of Mary's sisters jumped into the discussion. "Christmas is for families. It brings us all up to date as we share in the Lord's birth."

From Mary's place I went to the Wyncote Church Home. That's where I found Mabel and Carl in the hairdresser's shop. Since Mabel was under the dryer and Carl was waiting at the end of the line, I began with Carl. Carl really liked the candies and cookies sent by the women, so all he could focus on at that moment was what a good job the women had done. "When Christmas is over," Carl told me, "I'll still remember how nice the cakes and candies were." But when I kept pressing my question, Carl finally said, "Christmas means being a faithful member of the church." Then Carl repeated his belief that church membership can save us from isolation and the pain of our own sorrow.

Mabel, who at age ninety-five is our oldest member, was quick to respond to my request for her insight into the meaning of Christmas. "Christmas means a little bit of happiness now," she said joyously. Mabel had just moved into the Wyncote Home the week before and was "tickled to death" by her new surroundings. "In this place I have no worries," she continued. "I like the food, and I feel I'm being cared for." What a lovely turnaround for Mabel, who had become blind quite quickly during the past year! The sudden blindness had frustrated and depressed her, so I was happy to find her so positive and cheerful in her new home.

My week of visits continued, and in each place I was given an immediate and faith-filled response to my question. Hilda's answer revealed her good and generous spirit. "Christmas is about great joy. It's a day to look forward to for a long time." Vera commented on the mood of the season. "There's such lovely music. And people are much kinder. They talk to you and wish you 'Merry Christmas,' even in my place where most residents are Jewish." Then in a more serious tone she added, "Christmas is about rebirth—our rebirth."

I was impressed by the comments of our senior members. All gave different answers; no one hesitated. Their responses were genuine and spontaneous and revealed their long years of faithful living. Even though we don't get to see or interact with these homebound members of our congregation much, they are still very connected with us and very committed to their faith. In fact, some of them join us Sunday mornings for eleven o'clock worship by reading the service in the church bulletin we mail weekly.

Actually these senior members of our congregation link us with the tradition of Anna and Simeon, who were steadfast in their worship of God in the Temple. These two were righteous and devout people, scripture tells us, who believed in God's promise to send a Messiah. When Joseph and Mary enter the Temple with Jesus, both Simeon and Anna see the child and praise God for him. Guided by the Holy Spirit, they predict his destiny will be great. Simeon warns Mary, however, that not everyone will follow her son's leadership. She can expect him to be the center of great controversy and will herself go through great sorrow on account of his rejection.

Simeon then sings a beautiful song of praise, one that is a bit haunting in its mood, as it serves as a personal prayer of peaceful and joyful departure for Simeon. In it Simeon praises God for letting him see the promised Messiah, and then he asks for release from his Temple duties. In other words, Simeon articulates his own readiness to die, now that God's promise has been fulfilled in his life. It's almost as though Simeon recognizes in the birth of Jesus the completion of his purpose for living.

Simeon sings these poignant words:

> Master, now you are dismissing your servant in peace,
>   according to your word;
> for my eyes have seen your salvation,
>   which you prepared in the presence of all peoples,
> a light for revelation to the Gentiles
>   and for glory to your people Israel.[19]

Two of my pre-Christmas visits were with men facing death. Both were hospitalized. With one, I was not able to have a coherent conversation. But I offered him communion, and I do believe he understood what it was, because he accepted it, even though that day he had refused all liquids, as well as his medication. The other man was much more philosophical and in fact reviewed his whole spiritual life for me. At age nine he had experienced profound physical healing and never forgot it. "Whenever something is wrong," this man confessed, "the memory of that healing flashes before me." Somehow that healing of long ago still sustained his hope, even though his current situation was one of physical deterioration and discomfort. I marveled at his confident joy.

The strong faith of the senior members of our church encouraged me as I went about my visits. It is remarkable to discover the maturity of their witness, even in the waning hours of their lives. The joy of their faith is anything but naive optimism or superficial sentiment. Their faith has had to come to terms with sorrow and death. Their witness points beyond the circumstances of their lives to an unshakable joy and peace.

Meister Eckhart, the fourteenth-century mystic, once wrote, "When you reach the point where . . . sorrow is not sorrow for you, and where all things are a pure kind of peace for you, then a child is really born."[20]

I celebrated this kind of birth as I listened to the insights and inspiration of our seniors. Their vision, their joy and hope, enrich and balance the joy our children express. Christmas is not only for children; it is also for those who are shut in, as well as for those who are shut out, for the sick and the sorrowful, for those who are ending life, as well as for those who are beginning it. Christmas offers us new birth, at whatever stage we find ourselves.

EPIPHANY

A Wise Man Returns

As I usually do every Sunday, I began the children's sermon on Epiphany Sunday by inviting the children present to come forward to the chancel area. As expected, the children rushed forward, each one vying for a seat on the special sheep stool.

The children were eagerly telling me all about their favorite Christmas presents, while Nate, dressed in one of the Magi costumes from Christmas Eve, walked slowly up the center aisle behind the children. He was muttering something about the baby.

"Is he here? Have you seen the baby? I've looked everywhere, and I don't know where to find him. I thought he might be here."

As Nate got closer to the chancel I thought one of the children would blow his cover and yell out "Daddy." Nate's two young sons, who had not been told about the guest, were seated among the children. Instead they took the whole encounter quite seriously.

"Is he here? Have you seen the baby?" the stranger repeated directly to the children.

"Yes, he's here," the children shouted. "You've come to the right place."

I was amazed. Nate and I had worked out the story, sure that the children at best would be shy and confused and unable to answer with any certainty. But they were clear: The baby Jesus is here, among us!

So I pushed the question a bit. "Really?" I asked. "Well, where is he? Is he here hiding among us?"

"No!"

"Could he be out there in the congregation?"

"No!"

"Might he be sleeping under one of the pews?"

"No," they responded. At this point it was becoming a game.

"Well, where is he?" I asked once again. "Are you sure he is here, in our church?"

"Yes," they clamored in unison.

"Well, where is he then? This wise man wants to know."

One of the children exclaimed, "He's downstairs in the nursery!"

"Oh," I said, taken aback. "Could you show the wise man where the baby Jesus is?"

"Oh, yes," they all agreed. So as the congregation sang the next hymn, the children led the stranger downstairs to our nursery to see the baby Jesus.

I couldn't believe the dialogue that had just occurred. When most adults are not sure where to find Jesus, when there are so many different voices, each claiming to possess the truth about Jesus, when most Christians are in a state of confusion about their faith, our children are clear. Even several Sundays after Christmas, they are still sure that Jesus is among us.

When you think about it, it does seem perfectly logical. Try any church, any Sunday. Surely the baby Jesus can be found in the nursery!

Baptism in the Shelter

He stopped me in the hallway one evening and said, "Reverend, I want to be baptized. What do I have to do?" Since I had never noticed Leonard at any of our worship services, I wanted to know more. I wanted to know what had led him to this decision.

He told me that he had been present at our special Christmas Day service and had been quite moved by the singing of "I Wonder As I Wander" by "that lovely woman." The lovely woman is Priscilla, our soprano soloist, who on Christmas Day traditionally sings this Appalachian carol dressed as a homeless woman. Her singing always touches the hearts of both the homeless and those who work with them, as we gather on this holy day to celebrate Christ's birth. The words of the carol draw us in:

> I wonder as I wander, out under the sky,
> How Jesus the Savior did come for to die
> For poor ord'nary people like you and like I;
> I wonder as I wander, out under the sky.[21]

We are reminded that the one who had "nowhere to lay his head" came to be present among the least of us. Even the most distant and unbelieving are included.

Now I was beginning to understand Leonard's desire to receive the gift for himself, to "take on Christ" in this direct way. But baptism is also about becoming part of a new community, the church, and I had no idea what that might mean for Leonard. So I told him that I had to talk to the elders of the church and that I would like him to attend a regular service of worship on the coming Sunday. We had to get better acquainted.

A few days after the service we met with Joanna and Bob, two of the elders, and Leonard told us a little about his life. One of eighteen children, he was born in South Philadelphia, and, though his family was Roman Catholic, his mother had neglected to have him baptized. Now he was very clear: at age sixty-six he did not want to go to hell. Looking to the end of his life, he realized that salvation comes from God, and he didn't want to miss out on the gift. We probed a bit further. Did he know Jesus? Had he ever read the Bible? What part of it was "good news" for him?

"Oh, yes, I've read the Bible over and over," Leonard replied. "When I was in prison, I was often in solitary confinement, and there I read the Bible. I know the story of Jesus." And Leonard began to quote the stories that meant the most to him. It was obvious to Joanna, Bob, and me that Leonard was indeed acquainted with Jesus in a way many of us had never been. Leonard had been in prison for twenty-eight years, beginning at age fourteen. Our conversation finally ended with Leonard's plea: "Please don't make me wait too long."

The elders agreed to honor Leonard's request and asked that he attend worship the next Sunday and then meet regularly with two sponsors who would stand with him for the baptism.

If Leonard felt at home in our community, we would welcome him. There was only one warning the elders offered: "Don't expect the external circumstances of your life to change dramatically." They cautioned, "Baptism will connect you with a source of interior strength and with a new community of support and encouragement, but it doesn't mean all your problems will vanish. In fact, they might worsen. Baptism will not magically remove all your troubles; however, through baptism you might find a way to deal with them."

In the next couple of weeks I got to learn more about Leonard's life. He had been on the street for a long time, and one day when an outreach worker was trying to convince a man in an abandoned house to come into a shelter and get cleaned up, Leonard appeared and asked if he could come too. He was dressed in five or six coats, his hair was long and matted, and his face was unshaven. He heard the invitation in a personal way and accepted it. After a shower, shave, and haircut, Leonard took a good, long look in the mirror, and he liked what he saw. To be sure, Leonard is a very handsome man!

Baptism day came quickly, and early that morning Leonard was deep in prayer. Janet and Harvey, his two sponsors, arrived to sit with him. At the proper time, they accompanied him to the communion rail. Determined to give him all the support they could, they joined hands with him, one on either side, throughout the time he stood before the congregation. If only I had had enough water to baptize Leonard by immersion! Leonard was so eager for a total change, a new direction, a letting go of evil's power to control him, that I longed for something more dramatic than sprinkling a few drops of water on his head. Something new was happening to all of us.

Leonard's presence turned out to be a gift for our whole church. Because he had been sleeping in our social hall for some weeks, Leonard felt very much at home in our space. As we watched how easily he moved around our church kitchen, we learned that he had had experience as a chef. We were discovering lots of ways he could be part of the work of our church.

But in the next weeks Leonard's growing discomfort with his life became more and more apparent. He threatened to go back to live in the subway. He became intolerant of the behavior of the other men in the shelter. He found it easy to argue with the shelter supervisors. He was impatient with the circumstances of his life and longed for solitude, time by himself, even if that meant staying in the deep recesses of the subway. We presented options and encouraged him to stop drinking. And then Leonard disappeared. No one knew where he had gone. All our efforts to inquire about his whereabouts turned up no clues.

The Gospels say that, following Jesus' baptism, the Spirit immediately drove Jesus out into the wilderness where he was tempted by Satan. It seemed that the same thing was happening to our newly baptized member. I cannot help but wonder whether Leonard will survive the wilderness experience. May God's holy angels watch over him.

Transfigured by a Halo

Sometimes things happen so quickly. I was standing at the top of the stairs leading to our second-floor church sanctuary on a Sunday morning before worship. People were coming and going. The ushers were busy seating worshipers. Children were looking for their parents. Visitors were hesitantly arriving, looking for a comfortable spot in the sanctuary.

Then Charlie arrived. He had spent some months in our shelter, but he had since moved on to more permanent housing. "I'd like to show you something," he said amid all the hubbub of that Sunday morning. He pulled a photograph out of a brown envelope. "This is what I used to look like."

I gazed at the black-and-white photo, hardly recognizing the man who was in it. He had a long white beard, long hair, and a halo attached to his head.

I knew that Charlie had worn a halo for several months after he had fractured his skull. I had also heard that he hadn't wanted to have the halo removed, even after his skull had healed. It had served such a good purpose in Charlie's efforts at panhandling. When people saw the halo, they immediately dug into their pockets for loose change. Truly, as I looked at the photo I saw a resemblance with another homeless man who had lived two thousand years ago, only his halo had been a crown of thorns. No wonder people were quick to respond. But the halo had to come off, because the screws were going to become permanently embedded in his flesh.

Worship was about to begin. I didn't have a chance to make any comment. I just stood there in awe of the changes that had come to Charlie during these past months. What courage it must have taken for him finally to allow the halo to be removed.

The story of Jesus' transfiguration is a difficult one for us to grasp. When we stand with the disciples on the Mount of Transfiguration, we get a fleeting glimpse of Jesus in the shimmering light of the resurrection. It is a brief moment of awareness, but the image lasts. It serves as insight for the disciples who don't really understand the suffering that is to come to Jesus.

I had seen something similar in the photo from Charlie's past, but in reverse. Here was a man who had gone through the suffering of the cross. He had overcome dependency on his victim status and had claimed a different way of life. He had trusted the people who wanted to help him. Change was possible for Charlie. The resurrection can happen to us all. Transformation brings with it a whole new life. The image from the past served as a strong reminder of how much Charlie was living in the light of the resurrection right now!

LENT

Palm Sunday Guests

Palm Sunday is a very special day at Old First. The church sanctuary is decorated with two large palm trees, there's usually a trumpet to make the occasion especially festive, and the children are involved in welcoming everyone. Palm Sunday is a time when we celebrate our faith in very human terms. It is a day when we have little trouble relating to the message. We want victory, and we want it according to our expectations. Palm Sunday is also the beginning of Holy Week, so in the background looms the cross and the much more somber mood of Good Friday.

Palm Sunday is one of the Sundays when we invite our friends to worship with us. Our goal is to double the size of our congregation that morning. We specifically want to invite people who have a church background but who do not currently have a church home. By asking our friends to join us for the beginning of Holy Week, we are offering an invitation to return for the rest of the holiday season. Our hope is that some of our visitors might eventually consider joining our congregation.

One particular "Bring a Friend" Sunday was especially memorable. I was already beginning the sermon when Charlie and Gus appeared at the narthex door. Just as I got started, I saw them coming down the center aisle. "Oh no," I thought to myself. "These two." I knew them well. Gus and Charlie tended to drink too much and could easily get boisterous. They had few inhibitions and were capable of shouting out right in the middle of the sermon. What would I do then?

Since there was no room at the back of the sanctuary, Charlie and Gus came right down front. Everyone was watching them. I was praying real hard, even while I was preaching. They weaved their way to a front pew, confirming that they were under the influence of alcohol. Their ruddy complexions and tattered clothes contrasted with the spring finery of our members and guests. They managed to find seats and sat quietly throughout the rest of the service. I was glad for that. But I was wondering how our invited friends might react to these two "uninvited" guests.

Later that week I had a challenging conversation with an active member who appeared at my office door to object to our homeless visitors.

"Geneva," she began as she sat down next to my desk, "if you want this church to grow, you're going to have to stop the homeless from coming on Sunday mornings. We're tired of seeing them everywhere. We meet them on every street corner. They're always harassing us. Now we have to encounter them at church. They smell, they're obnoxious, they're always drunk, they're annoying, and we're tired of them. We come to church to worship God, and we can't do that with these people everywhere. If you want to get new members, you'll have to get rid of the homeless. New members don't want this kind of hassle. They want to worship in peace. They don't want to be reminded of these dirty, embarrassing people."

I was taken aback. Here I was, face-to-face with someone

who was going to make me choose between two goals: the growth of our congregation and the mission of our church. I didn't want to choose. I wanted both. But she was making me take sides. I couldn't avoid it. So I took a deep breath and began.

"I'm sorry," I said, "but I have to take my stand with Jesus. That's whom I've chosen to follow, and Jesus hung out with sinners and outcasts and unclean people. They were his friends. We are a church. We have to keep our doors open to everyone, and that includes the homeless. I can't ask them to leave, and I don't want anyone else to do so either." I was adamant. I was not even open to compromise. It was very clear to me.

My visitor continued. "I know someone who was here last Sunday who was very offended by Gus. She felt he was uncouth, and I agree with her. You shouldn't let these homeless people get too close to you. We don't like it."

Again I stated my position. "The homeless are part of my ministry here in the neighborhood; I can't ignore them."

"I see," she said, and stood up to leave my office.

Again I reaffirmed my position. When my visitor had gone, I was left to think about her comments. I could not have given any other response.

Later that week, I received the following letter from a friend of the church who had attended our Palm Sunday service:

Just a short note to say thanks for a most meaningful Palm Sunday service. I was very impressed by the visitors who came for "Bring a Friend" Sunday. I was also impressed with the homeless who made me feel a little uncomfortable, as they should. In this respect I recognize that the Palm Sunday message is for "all," and not just for middle-class people like me.

When we open our doors to welcome friends, we might even find that the "friends of Jesus" come inside too.

Church growth happens in all kinds of ways. A couple of years later, I discovered that the woman who had objected to our Palm Sunday visitors had signed up to make a homecooked meal for the men of our shelter. She was growing, and so is our church.

An Offensive Jesus

The newspaper account said that "the crucifix-sculpture caused quite a controversy when it appeared three weeks ago outside the Old First Reformed Church. There were those who thought the piece to be a mockery of religion, and there were those who found the piece inspiring because of its very grotesqueness. It isn't there now though, because it was ripped from the cross and stolen Friday night."[22]

Horrible. Hideous. Horrendous. What was so offensive about the skinny red-vinyl figure that someone would decide to take it down from the cross?

The artist, Larry Moog, a member of the Bird and Dirt Collaborative, fashioned a twentieth-century Christ out of trash found in the alleys and doorways of abandoned buildings near the church. He wanted a Christ figure that was not male or female, black or white, young or old. The figure was to represent all humanity. It turned out to be a waif of a body with aluminum beads as hair, coconut shells for breasts, webbed feet, and sumac branches for arms. One thousand one-inch nails holding the vinyl body in place were arranged in ancient patterns to symbolize the Christ—the fish, the egg, the tree, and the Greek Chi-Rho. Clad only in a loincloth, the figure hung on the lonely corner for three weeks. The crown of thorns on its head was made weightier by cast-off spark plugs. And inside the chest of the corpus, purple, red, and yellow dye bled into the loincloth whenever rain struck the figure. Interaction with the natural environment was part of the effect the artist wanted the figure to have. But the figure's interaction with the *human* environment was even more noteworthy.

The figure was completed on Ash Wednesday and placed on the huge outdoor cross fashioned from some oaken trusses once used in the historic church building. The horizontal beam of the cross bore the words from "Battle Hymn of the Republic," updated to make them more inclusive: "He died to make *us* holy." There was no mistaking the intention. Passersby were immediately intrigued by the figure. It was controversial. It made one want to turn away. Church members were outspoken in their criticism of the sculpture. "This grotesque figure is at the center of our faith?" they wondered. One member, however, had a very different point of view.

Marion wrote down her response to the sculpture in a letter to the pastor. In it she reflected on the words of Isaiah 53.

> *"He was despised and rejected." That's it, you see, Jesus hung on the cross because the people of religion could not accept him. . . . The artist has made us participants in the drama of Calvary. He has shown us clearly that we, too, are capable of rejecting that which does not conform to our way of thinking, that which is a threat to our cherished images.*

One day when the pastor was away at a church meeting, someone pulled the body off the cross. Had there been a plot to take it down all along? Had someone paid to have it destroyed? Were church members involved? Slowly the facts emerged.

Sure enough, two church leaders had done the deed. When the pastor called them to the church, he read them the letter Marion had sent. They were so moved when confronted by biblical teaching that they decided to put the sculpture back up on "their" cross. Whereupon the pastor suggested that the artist reconfigure the piece on the cross. That's what happened.

However, sometime later, on a Friday evening, the pastor noticed that the cross was empty once again. After searching for pieces of the sculpture around the church building, he notified the news media, who reported the theft. Seeing the news article, a neighbor brought the head to the church. He had found it in the Fourth and Race intersection on Friday evening and had taken it home. It wasn't until he saw the article in *The Sunday Bulletin* that he realized what it was and hastened to return it. The head was refastened to the cross, where it remained until the sculpture was taken down during the Good Friday service.

An offensive Jesus. Who would have guessed that the tiny baby would grow up to confront us in this way. Jesus continues to stretch our imagination as the cuddly child in the manger turns into the stark figure on barren Calvary. Perhaps Simeon's prophetic words to Mary at the presentation of the infant Jesus in the Temple in Jerusalem ring true: This child will be "a sign that will be opposed so that the inner thoughts of many will be revealed. . . ."[23]

Holy Week Experiences

It was Monday night of Holy Week. I was already in bed when the telephone rang. The supervisor of our church's shelter for the homeless was on the other end of the line. "There's a loud bell ringing over here, and we don't know how to shut it off. Sorry to bother you, but could you stop by?"

I could hear the sound over the telephone and recognized it as the front doorbell of our church. "Now how could the doorbell be stuck?" I wondered. It seemed strange, but there was no mistaking the loud ringing sound.

In a hurry I threw on my clothes and a minute later arrived at the church. By this time several of the men from the shelter were carrying containers of water around to the side of the building. I followed them to see what was happening. Then I saw the smoke and flames. Someone had piled garbage up against the side of our more than 150-year-old building and set the trash bags on fire. Fortunately for us, the doorbell wire ran along the edge of the wooden windowsill, and the flames had shorted the wire, setting off the bell.

Although the bell alerted those inside, a passerby had already spotted the flames and called the fire department. We heard the sirens, and in a few minutes the big red trucks pulled up. By now there were enough people outside to direct the firefighters to the spot. In a few seconds they had connected their long hoses to the fire hydrant and quickly extinguished the fire. Then they went down under the church building to make sure the fire was completely out. Soon they were off.

The shelter supervisor, some of the men who had carried buckets of water, and I were left to survey the damage and collect our thoughts. How could something like this have happened? The fire clearly had been intentionally set. Who was responsible for such a terrible act? Why would anyone want to set our church on fire?

Already the supervisor and the men had figured it out. There had been a fight at the shelter the night before, and three men had been asked to leave. They were upset and had threatened to burn down the church building in retaliation. Some of the other men had overheard their threats, and those who made the threats had been seen near the church earlier in the evening.

What to do now? The staff had to deal with the men who were suspected of starting the fire; I had to worry about the church building. How would the trustees react? It would be easy for them to close the shelter after something like this.

I went back again to the place where the fire had been set. It was obvious that the fire had had the potential of being serious. The flames had reached within inches of an old wooden window frame. If the doorbell wire underneath the windowsill had not shorted, more damage might have been done. Before they left, the firefighters removed blackened trash from the side of the building, revealing a large area beneath the window that had been scarred by soot.

What would the trustees say? How might I break the news to them? How could I respond to their fears? They certainly would be tempted to close down the entire shelter operation.

We were glad to help the homeless, but we were not ready to risk destruction of our historic church building. I could anticipate the reaction of the trustees, and I could appreciate their position.

But it was also Holy Week. How could we expect to open ourselves to our city's wounded ones and not have scars to show on our body, our building? What makes us think Christ's body should be safe from the violent motives of people in our day? Christ was on trial during Holy Week, headed for the cross.

The next day I showed the blackened spot to Bill, the janitor of our church. Perhaps his reaction to what happened might give me a clue in approaching the trustees. Bill tended to be supercautious; he was not likely to take risks with unreliable people.

Bill was surprised by what had happened. But he just shook his head and said, "Okay, I'll get a bucket and some soap and water and see if I can clean off the bricks." He was also willing to shovel the debris from the fire into plastic garbage bags and haul it away.

I then proceeded to telephone the trustees. I was able to tell them not only about the incident, but also about our cleanup efforts. And I had to ask one of them to repair the doorbell wire. Earl, head of the trustees, said he would come to the church shortly to look over the situation. Meanwhile Bill had already begun to wash the bricks.

I was proud of the reaction of our church trustees. They went about helping the janitor clean up, and soon the doorbell wire was fixed. There was no reaction of anxiety or fear or panic on their part. They didn't think of closing down the shelter, and I didn't mention it either.

Now I had to go to the men in the shelter. We had to talk. I had to make sure they were aware of what a serious incident the fire had been. I wanted to discuss the consequences of taking anger out on the church building. We had to renew the unspoken trust the church had extended to the men by allowing them to come into our building in the first place.

Later that week, on Good Friday evening, I was at home when a knock came at my door. I wasn't expecting anyone, so I opened it with a bit of caution. Some of the men from the shelter were standing there.

"We'd like you to come over to the shelter for a little while. It's Good Friday, and we'd like you to pray with us. We really need it," one of them said quite unapologetically.

I was very moved. The fire had made an impression on them. They were beginning to realize what is at risk in our life together. And so our weekly prayer sessions began.

When we first opened our church social hall as a temporary winter shelter, we didn't want to make the men repay us by listening to sermons; we just wanted to provide a warm place for them. Whenever our church responds to the needs of others, it does so without asking anything in return. Later we added hot coffee and food, showers and clean clothes, and support services, such as counseling, medical assistance, and additional housing options. Last of all, we thought of praying with the men. Or rather, they thought of it first and requested it of us.

The prayer sessions have been going on every week since that first Good Friday. Of all the contact I have had with the men over the years, praying with them has been the most real and rewarding part of our relationship. In the sessions, the men open everything to God. They don't hold back. Sometimes they listen to one another and try to address some of the concerns that are raised. But mostly they unabashedly express their deepest wishes and fears, almost in stream-of-consciousness conversation. Each of them speaks directly to God.

I am amazed at the wide range of topics that are raised in these prayer sessions. There's always a great deal of concern for family and loved ones. Even though these men's lives are often filled with experiences of alienation from family relationships, family is usually foremost on everyone's mind. There's a lot of unresolved grief and sadness and guilt about not being a better son or husband or father. But there's also joy in the prayer sessions, and always thanksgiving for the blessings of life itself and for those who have reached out to them in kindness. Then there are those amazing prayers for unknown people—the suffering in Africa, the victims of violence on our city's streets, the children and teachers in our schools, medical staff at nearby hospitals, members of the congregation. One man always prays for "the intentions of those who are not able to be present."

The supervisor and volunteers join in too. There is a wonderful leveling, as we all come before God in our common need. My heart is often moved and strengthened by the witness these men make. In their poverty, the men are not really aware of the spiritual riches they communicate.

Sometimes people ask me whether we require the men of our shelter to study the Bible. Do we evangelize them? I really like being asked this question, because in fact it is the homeless who evangelize us. They are the ones who share the good news of God's love so readily. They don't hold back. They are able to share freely the joy of knowing that they have been blessed by

God. I always smile when one of the men starts to preach to me. "Go on," I mutter under my breath. How I need to hear the truth of God's love, fresh from their experience!

Out of a potentially tragic situation of betrayal and revenge, from the ashes of a Holy Week fire, a new relationship of trust and openness between the church and our homeless guests has emerged. We are closer now, for we all understand the risk involved in our connectedness. Because we lived the paschal mystery so intensely that one Holy Week, we are now able to honor the presence of God's renewing grace at the center of our acquaintance throughout the years.

A See-through Jesus

Who is this Jesus? We know him as someone who is at once common and ordinary and yet startles us with his miraculous healing power and amazingly perceptive presence. We meet him in scripture as teacher, healer, prophet, friend, liberator, and brother. We see him as sometimes demanding and confronting; at other times, compassionate, generous, appreciative, warm-hearted, encouraging, full of joy! Never do we expect to see him on a cross—his face shattered, his clothes torn, his body bruised and battered.

The picture we have of Jesus on Good Friday is shocking. He is not your typical hero. Who would have thought it would have come to this? Our hope was for a much more successful and promising leader. How can we believe in someone who appears so weak, so pathetically vulnerable?

On Good Friday we see Jesus on the cross, betrayed by a friend, abandoned by disciples, condemned by the authorities, misunderstood by the crowd—and yes, it seems, even forsaken by God. The Gospel accounts of Christ's passion confront us with a man who was broken in both body and spirit. He was silenced—emptied of all power and joy, rejected and neglected, alone—completely alone on the cross.

This is what strikes me about the see-through Jesus hanging on the cross in our church courtyard. It was created by Father Dennis McNally, a St. Joseph's University fine arts professor, from thin netting, shaped into bodily form. At first we hardly notice the figure in the busyness of city life. Christ's body seems lost in the rush of things, foolishly transparent to the world's ways. It isn't until we stop and take a long second look that we realize just who this image is. Then we might feel the weight of the body, the strain on the neck; we might even hear the scream.

Father McNally told me about a little boy he saw who came up to the figure on the cross and began to punch at it. Then he kicked the body. It moved. When Father McNally asked him whether he had hit it, the boy answered, "Oh no!" But his sister said, "Yes, he did!"

On Palm Sunday church members decorated the body with colorful ribbons. It looked so festive. But during the week all the ribbons got tangled up inside the body, and the image of the man hanging there became fuzzy and blurred. We couldn't see him very clearly. But later in the week the wind started to stir the ribbons, and the body began to move and twist and turn and take on a new kind of power.

What can we say about this person Jesus? When we first look at him we see straight through him. He seems to embrace the emptiness from which we so readily flee. But then we discover a strange power in what at first appeared so vulnerable. The words of the apostle Paul help us: "For the message about the cross is foolishness to those who are perishing, but to us who are being saved it is the power of God. . . . Has not God made foolish the wisdom of the world? . . . For God's foolishness is wiser than human wisdom, and God's weakness is stronger than human strength."[24]

Maybe now we can proclaim faith in this transparent man of whom the Roman centurion, facing the cross and watching Jesus breathe his last breath, said, "Truly this man was God's child!"[25]

The Shattered Christ

*

"Is that a target behind the cross in your church courtyard?" someone asked me. "Wow." His eyes opened wide as his imagination led him to reflect on the full impact of the target and of Jesus, hanging there at dead center, shattered into multiple mirror fragments on the cross.

"The Shattered Christ" was the title of one year's winning entry in our lenten art competition. Suzanne Ellis, who created the contemporary depiction of the crucifixion displayed on our outdoor cross, commented about her piece: "The shattered Christ figure in mirror, inlaid on a gold cross on top of a striking black firing target, to me epitomizes the enduring, redeeming figure of Christ in an era of mindless violence. Christ can be seen in the foreground of the piece, barring the use of the target and by extension condemning indiscriminate violence."

The violence of our day depicted on the cross, projected onto the central symbol of our faith, moves us to reflect on how it is that violence seems to have run amok, not just in our city, but throughout our country and the world.

Everywhere life seems to be caught up in a violence that seeks to destroy the beauty and truth and goodness around it. From pollution that attacks the environment to the random shooting of innocent children on the streets of our city, violence everywhere seems to have us in its grip. There seems to be no safe place, nowhere to hide from the danger. So many innocent people seem to be at the center of the target: passersby, people minding their own business, people simply born into a community where poverty is the way of life. The violence of our day has many victims. It is so pervasive. It doesn't seem fair that so many people are affected by its deadly power.

Sooner or later we all feel the effects of violence gone wild. Fear paralyzes us. Anger wells up within. We want to do something, but it all seems so far beyond our power to control. Bitterness, cynicism, utter frustration take over and isolate us from any organized response. We all become victims of a society that produces too many weapons and refuses drastically to curtail their use. The very freedom we enjoy in this country ironically fires back at us when the inner control of a common moral code is lacking from our national character and purpose.

"My God, my God, why have you forsaken us?" we wonder. The cry of Jesus from the cross becomes our cry as we, people of goodwill and compassion, ponder the future of a country in which trust and cooperation are being held captive to personal freedom and individual rights. Where will it end? Can it ever be brought under control? Why doesn't God do something?

We all want easy answers, clear solutions. Does it really help us when we contemplate Jesus' violent death on a cross? Does it make any difference when we realize that God permitted Jesus—God's own child—to die at the hands of powerful conspirators? Is there any comfort in knowing that Jesus was convicted by false testimony? Couldn't the crowd have been brought under control? What about Pilate? He ruled with the authority of the powerful Roman Empire. Surely he could have decided differently. Why didn't God do something? That's the question of Good Friday.

That's what they all said as they mocked Jesus on the cross. "He saved others; he cannot save himself. Let the Messiah, the Ruler of Israel, come down from the cross now, so that we may see and believe."[26]

During the last days of Lent, as I moved around that outdoor cross in our church courtyard, as I looked at it under various circumstances, as I glanced up at the shattered figure at different times of the day and night, I had two reactions.

The first one was "broken Jesus," who hangs on the cross seemingly so weak, unable to change anything. There were times when the mirror material of the body seemed to reflect life around it, showing so starkly the fragmented, powerless lives we all lead. The cold starkness of the corpus seemed to hang there, defying the power of any human strategy to make a difference.

But there were other, less frequent times when the figure on the cross seemed to absorb and take unto itself all the pain of human life around it. Jesus, hanging there in dignity, accepting the pain, redeeming the suffering, brings together the whole world through his dying body. This weak figure in the end becomes strong Jesus. All the fragmentation our world endures is made whole in Jesus' death. Through his vulnerability on the cross, Jesus brings hope and consolation to us in our afflictions, new direction and purpose to us in our human failures, healing and redemption to us, even in our sinful, broken nature.

It seems contradictory to all human wisdom. It seems foolish to think in these terms. Yet, for us who are being saved, here is the real power of God. To paraphrase the apostle Paul, the world did not know God through wisdom, but on the cross the world saw that the foolishness of God is wiser than human wisdom, that the weakness of God is stronger than human strength.[27] Herein lies our hope, herein lies our healing, herein lies our salvation. Herein lies the goodness of the lenten season.

The Sheltering Cross

I've always thought of the cross as a place of suffering and pain, a place of torture and cruelty, a place of execution and death. And that it is. It is the place where the ways of the world finally overcome the goodness of God's own child. But the cross can look quite different when viewed through the eyes of those who have been abandoned. Seen from the perspective of those who have been abused and rejected, the cross takes on a much more hopeful meaning.

Jesus said: "Come to me, all you who are weary and are carrying heavy burdens, and I will give you rest. . . . Learn from me; for I am gentle and humble in heart, and you will find rest for your souls."[28]

The cross, seen in its horizontal dimension, can be quite inviting. It can be the last place of refuge and comfort because the One who died on it knew the hopelessness and abandonment of those who have been rejected and regarded as disposable. The outstretched arms of the cross open wide to receive all those who have no other place to go.

Thomas Merton once wrote: "We live in a time of no room. . . . Into this world, this demented inn, in which there is absolutely no room for Him at all, Christ has come uninvited. But because He cannot be at home in it, and yet he must be in it, His place is with those others for whom there is no room."[29]

Merton's words were the inspiration for Sister Helen David's artpiece "The Sheltering Cross," which was on display as our outdoor lenten cross for two weeks prior to Good Friday. Sister Helen David commented that "the homeless are the living cross of our city, our nation. This piece places the homeless of all races in front of us as icons of suffering. The stranger, the Christ, is with them, is one of them."

Sister Helen David based her figures on real people she had met at St. John's Hospice, one of several places offering shelter and food to the abandoned poor of our city. It is only eight blocks from our church.

To create the figures around the cross she used new rough wood. "The homeless were not born weathered; they were battered by circumstances of life," she explained. Teenagers and adults at her Community Art Center in Southwest Philadelphia helped her pound and desecrate the new planks of wood. They applied scratches, paint spills, hammer poundings, chisel marks, stains—just as individuals sometimes mistreat others. Then the images were painted with regular house paint and the wood stained so the marks showed through. As the artpiece stood outdoors for several weeks, it was subjected to all kinds of weather conditions that further damaged the work. The wood planks warped slightly, and the paint cracked.

The homeless were mysteriously present when Sister Helen David came to install her work. How did they know about it? There they were, gathered from around the neighborhood to see this new object on the urban landscape. And they were quick to interpret its message. "What I get out of it," one man said, "is that Jesus is on the same level as the homeless. No matter if you are in a dark alley, or in a dumpster, Jesus is right there with you. In your darkest night, Jesus is there. In rain or snow, in sleet or wind, Jesus walks with you."

At the birth of Jesus there was no room in the inn, but at his death on the cross, there is plenty of room. Good Friday stands Thomas Merton's words on their head. Ironically there *is* room at the cross—plenty of room for all those who have been cast aside. The arms of the cross open wide to receive the multitude.

Another homeless man who viewed Sister Helen David's work summed up the hopefulness of the sheltering cross with these words: "The strength that guides this world cannot be stopped. There's an upward pull that is very powerful." As I thought about it, I realized that not only does the horizontal crossbeam embrace the marginalized, but the vertical beam contains a greater hope. Already in its vertical dimension, the cross anticipates the resurrection. In the cross of Jesus Christ then, the incarnation is complete; it points to the ultimate reconciliation of God and the world.

A Dead Tree Blossoms

Isaiah tells us:

> . . . he grew up before him like a young plant,
>   and like a root out of dry ground;
> he had no form or majesty . . . ,
>   nothing in his appearance that we should desire him.
> He was despised and rejected by others;
>   a man of suffering and acquainted with
>   infirmity; . . . [30]

It is difficult to look at the form on the cross—especially for Protestants. We are used to seeing a cross that has been freed of its dying corpse. We want our cross to be a symbol of the resurrection, of the freedom and new life found there.

But during the days of Lent and Holy Week it is important to remember that a real person struggled and suffered, that a real person died and gave up his life on the cross. Otherwise Easter doesn't really have much meaning. We can't enter into its joy very deeply if we haven't faced the horror of the crucifixion and the finality of Good Friday. This is one reason why we ask artists to help us feel and experience the crucifixion through a contemporary expression of the cross installed outdoors in our church courtyard during the days preceding Good Friday.

One year, Margaret Thompson, a Sister of St. Joseph and assistant professor at Moore College of Art and Design, constructed a figure for our cross made of two fallen tree limbs she had found in a nearby city park. Very carefully she joined them together to form an elongated body, wrapped the corpus with scraps of white cloth, and sealed the body with wax. Then she hung the form on our outdoor cross. Against the drape of a purple cloth the body looked like an ashen, ghostlike figure.

By day cars parked up close to the figure in our courtyard, crowding it out so that you could barely see its outstretched body on the cross. It seemed to be squeezed tightly into the midst of our congested urban lives. But at night, when no one was around, the body seemed lonely, so abandoned, hanging there in the snow, the rain, and the wind.

As I passed by the elongated white body stretched out on the lenten cross, I felt as if I were looking straight into the wound of our contemporary world. At first I thought of the woundedness of nature, polluted and destroyed by ever-present chemicals. Knowing that the body had been constructed from broken-off tree limbs, I related it first and foremost to the natural world from which it came. But because of its urban setting, right next to the parked cars, the woundedness of the city—beset by human loneliness and isolation—was painfully present to me as well. As I rushed by on my way to yet one more meeting, the never-ending demands and pressures of our contemporary lifestyles that stretch us beyond our human capacity, almost to the breaking point, seemed to be present too.

Can these dry boughs live again? I wondered. Can they come back to life? The wounds of our living seem to cut us off from the very source that gives life. Illness, depression, heavy burdens interfere and separate us from the vitality of our living. As people of faith who live in a world that is congested and alienated, we can easily feel dried up. Our enthusiasm drains away. We have no inspiration for living. There is no hope in us. All around us life seems brittle and barren. Where is the joy we used to know?

Deep at the center of our living is this wound, this vulnerability. Try as we might, it won't go away. It defies our control. We want to hide it, hoping no one else will notice, but the ache is there, the pain is real.

Good Friday is the day to look into that wound, to stare it in the face, to see it for what it really is, to acknowledge that we cannot fix it by ourselves. Good Friday is a day to look to the cross and through it find our hope. On this tree, the Savior of the world died, and by his death, by *his* wounds, we all are healed. How is it possible that one person's death might lead all of us to new life? That is the mystery of our faith, for we believe that by following this one person through death we will be brought out of it to life once more.

Nicola Slee, in a poem titled "Spring Trees at Pleshey," writes:

> And can these dry bones live?
> these bare boughs sprout green?
>
> and each stalk
> is sharp, dry as chalk,
> scratches blood
> with the hard knot of wood.

And can these dry boughs live?
Yes, since one tree of death
bore love's last breath . . .
and flamed with the fruit of Christ's risen body
on the first Good Sunday,
all trees on earth partake this miracle,
proclaim this glory.

Look, long, then, here, at this
budding of dead wood:

and in our lives,
however dry or gnarled the grain,
He'll cause the flower of love
to sprout again.[31]

The promise of the resurrection is real. I saw it outside on
the lenten cross. The miracle happened as the warm weather
forced the blossoms on the tree behind the stark figure to bloom
all at once. The lonely, ghostlike form on the cross no longer
stood by itself. Now it was encircled by the beauty of the white
blossoms from the pear tree nearby, which lives and has life
because its roots go deep and are connected to the soil from
which it draws nourishment. My question—"Can these dry
boughs live?"—was answered in the natural cycle of springtime.
I had thought there would be no solution to the brokenness I
had met on the cross, but now there was a natural, yet deeply
mysterious, response. And in it I found hope that the profound
questions of our contemporary world will find resolution too.

Can our wounded lives be made whole? Yes, in the blossoming Easter cross I found an answer!

Jesus said, "Abide in me as I abide in you. Just as the branch cannot bear fruit by itself unless it abides in the vine, neither can you unless you abide in me."[32] This is said by the living Christ to our hearts. We cannot bring forth the full fruits of the Christian life unless we are rooted and grounded and growing in the source of life.

Can these dry boughs live again? The answer lies in how deeply we bond with this Living One who died on the tree.

EASTER

A Resurrection Story, on the Run

On Good Friday, the lenten artpiece in our church courtyard comes down, and the plain wooden cross, with a black cloth draped over it, remains for Holy Saturday. Early on Easter morning, a beautiful spray of flowers is placed on that same cross. It greets the worshipers who arrive for our Easter dawn service, held around the courtyard cross.

There's much to do to set up for this early morning service. Folding chairs have to be carried outside. Hymnals and bulletins need to be distributed. And the floral arrangement has to be fastened to the cross. I usually ask some of the men from the shelter to help with these tasks. They're just finishing breakfast and preparing to leave for the day while I'm trying to set things up. Someone usually volunteers to hang the flowers. In the special atmosphere of early dawn, something as subtle as putting the flowers on the cross can make a homeless man feel very much a part of the Easter celebration.

One year it rained, and we had to move the service indoors, into the social hall. What a scramble! The men were finishing breakfast, and we were trying to set up for our early service and the traditional Easter breakfast that follows.

I wasn't sure whether anyone would remember to take the ladder outdoors in the pouring rain to put the flowers on the cross, but a man met me as he was returning the ladder to its usual spot. He commented very quietly, "Reverend, I want to thank you. This place was just what I needed. Tonight I'm heading out to a live-in job as a cook at a camp in the mountains. Staying here really got me through a hard time. Thanks again."

The conversation happened so quickly, and then the man disappeared. A resurrection story, told on the run, in the confusion of Easter dawn. Who says the resurrection has to be something big, bold, and flashy? We celebrated together as church members arrived and the homeless stayed on to sing "Today the grave has lost its sting. Alleluia!"[33]

At the Emmaus Table

I don't know where she came from. She seemed to appear out of nowhere. We had finished Sunday morning worship, and most of the church members were on their way home. A few of us remained, hoping to gather for some Bible study. But first we wanted to have lunch.

Suddenly the front door of the church opened and an older woman entered. She sat down on a bench in the narthex and demanded a sandwich. "I'm hungry. I want a sandwich," she said in quite a loud voice.

I knew we had plenty of sandwiches at our luncheon table, and if not, surely there were extra fixings in the kitchen to make another one. "Okay," I said, "I think I can find one for you."

Soon I returned with a sandwich and a cup of juice. The woman grabbed the sandwich out of my hand and stuck it into her mouth. She didn't touch the juice. A few minutes later she called out again.

"I'm hungry. I want a sandwich." Well, it was understandable; this woman looked very hungry. She appeared to have been out on the street for many days. Her skin, darkened by many hours in the sun, looked tough and leathery. Her unwashed hair seemed coarse and stringy. She definitely needed a bath. And her feet were swollen, a sure sign that she had been walking on the pavement for many days.

*

"Okay," I responded a second time. "I think I can find another sandwich for you." And sure enough, I returned with a second sandwich. Again, the woman snatched it out of my hand and stuck it in her mouth without a word.

"I'm hungry. I want a sandwich." In disbelief I went back to the kitchen to see if there was enough bread to make a third sandwich. Yolanda helped scrape together something, but the more I brought her, the more the stranger wanted. We had no bread left, yet the woman kept insisting. We tried ignoring her, but she moved in and joined us at our table, still demanding more bread. We were ready to begin the Bible study. Who was this woman? What was she doing in our church? Why was she asking for more and more bread, repeating her plea like a broken record?

We tried to find out her name, but she didn't respond to our questions. She just kept asking for bread. She seemed to be lost. We telephoned some of our friends who know many of the homeless people in the city. Perhaps she had wandered out of a shelter. Maybe someone was searching for her. But no one could identify her.

Finally one of our members walked her out to the bench in the narthex so we could begin Bible study. We heard her continue to ask for a sandwich as we began to study the passage about the two disciples who were on their way to the village of Emmaus when a stranger joined them. The stranger didn't seem to know what had happened early that morning in Jerusalem, but as they walked along the road, he interpreted the scriptures to them. Later when they were at table, breaking bread together, the two disciples recognized this stranger as the risen Christ. The story was all about seeing who the stranger really was.

Midway through our Bible study, someone went to the narthex to check on the stranger who had joined us at our luncheon table demanding bread. She was no longer there. She must have wandered off. We couldn't find her anywhere. But her presence, even for those few minutes, brought fresh perspective to our story of Jesus, at table breaking bread with two of his disciples in Emmaus and opening the scriptures to them.

Easter Monday,
but Still in the Tomb

*

There was a knock at my door early one Easter Monday morning. The desperate man who stood there was anything but a sign of the resurrection. I was into Easter, joyful, yet tired from the endless days of celebration that make up Holy Week and Easter Sunday. I was not expecting to see anyone still stuck on Good Friday.

Hungry and dirty, the young man pleaded for some food. "I haven't eaten in days," he offered as a word of explanation for his condition. The terrible tragedy of seeing this man in such a disheveled state on Easter Monday morning was that I knew him to be a gifted musician and painter. At one time he had been on our church's summer staff. It was he who had painted the large composite mural of the Tot Lot children that hangs in our social hall. I had known him under better circumstances. Even when he was confused and having mental problems and had a falling out with his father, he still managed to keep himself clean and neat. What had happened to make him seem so abandoned? He told me he had been staying in a shelter during recent weeks, ever since his nervous breakdown. Sensing my unspoken questions, he voluntarily tried to explain his new situation.

Had the resurrection happened? Where was the hope of Easter for this young man? There wasn't any sign of new life, not yet. How hard it was to stand by and realize what a long, long way there was to go before he would have a whole, a new, a healed life.

Looking at Easter from this side of the tomb, we expect the resurrection to come quickly. We are so impatient. We know how the story ends. We want the certainty of Easter now. How hard it is for us to wait for the resurrection. Ambiguity is something we'd rather not deal with.

In the freshness of Easter dawn, perhaps it is more realistic to be uncertain about what really happened. Perhaps it is important to wait and see how it all will come out in the end. Perhaps Mark's Gospel is right to leave us standing with the women at the empty tomb, frightened and trembling. We are unsure; the future seems ominous.

So it is for many people who face difficult circumstances. Neomi's father was hospitalized for several weeks as he slowly awoke from a stroke. With much effort and physical therapy he began to talk and move his limbs, to get out of bed, and to struggle to walk again. Steve, undergoing facial surgery after a senseless mugging in front of his home on Palm Sunday evening, was still thinking about the fragility of human life and the shock of having his future put at risk. Ellie, who had received a heart transplant during Holy Week, was still getting used to the miracle of having a second chance at happiness. For each one of them, new life was filled with uncertainties, fears, and the unknown. How will it all end?

Mark leaves us hanging there, just like life does. Mark refuses to tie together the loose ends of the Gospel into a tidy package of neat conclusions. Terror and amazement are the words he uses to sum up "the good news of Jesus Christ." Isn't this how Easter dawns upon us—with a mixture of promise and apprehension? Mark's ending leaves us hungry and haunted. We are sent back to read the story all over again, to search for clues about what Jesus really said, to ponder anew his life and ministry. Our exploration is just beginning. There is more to come.

Some years later the man who had come to my door on Easter Monday morning returned. I hadn't seen him for four years. This time I didn't recognize him right away. He had gained weight. He was well dressed. He looked very happy. He stopped by just to say hello and to let me know how well he was doing. He had gotten treatment for his illness, was on regular medication, and had been attending weekly therapy sessions. No longer staying in a shelter, he now had a small room in subsidized housing. He told me he was playing the piano again in a small restaurant and in his spare time painting portraits of his neighbors' children. It was great to see him, to witness this powerful sign of God's ability to heal and to bring someone back to life. The man was doing so well that occasionally, he told me, he returns to the shelter where he once lived to play the piano for the men. Then he added, quite as an aside, "You know, some of the men who were staying in the shelter four years ago are still there."

It takes a long time for most of us to get it. It takes a long time to experience healing and forgiveness and new life. It takes a long time for real change to happen. But what we do know, what Mark tells us beyond any shadow of a doubt, is that Jesus goes before us, preparing a way, opening the doors, standing there in his risen power, beckoning us on.[34]

Easter Monday and still in the tomb . . . death has a way of hanging around. It takes a long time for us to see that the stone has been rolled away and that we are free to get up and walk out into a new life.

At the Emmaus Table Again

Many years ago I spent the Easter holiday in France. While I was there I received a telegram from friends in Philadelphia. It said: "The world is a small village, and its name is Emmaus. Christ is risen!"

That telegram made me realize that on Easter Day we all find ourselves gathered in the same place, around the Emmaus table. We all come there as disciples, and in our confusion we recognize the risen Christ in the breaking of the bread.

I have always been fond of this biblical story about the things that happened to the two disciples as they walked with the stranger to the village of Emmaus on Easter evening. As a child I learned this story well, because I lived in an old Moravian town, named Emmaus in honor of the biblical one. It is located about fifty miles north of Philadelphia, near some other very old Moravian settlements named Bethlehem and Nazareth. When I became pastor of Old First, among the membership at that time was an elderly man who had also grown up in Emmaus and moved to Philadelphia many years before to teach at the University of Pennsylvania. His name was Claude.

The last time I saw Claude was a few days before his death; I visited him in a nursing home near Philadelphia. When I arrived Claude was a bit confused and seemed unsure about a number of things. His uncertainty was very much out of character, because as a scientist Claude had always exhibited a clear mind and calm sense of inner discretion. He was a very considerate person, gentle and understanding of others. His transparent blue eyes revealed the soul of a very wise and spiritual person. But when I entered his room on this particular day, Claude sat with his head bent down and his body slouched low in his chair.

It appeared that it was not going to be easy to carry on a coherent conversation, so I immediately began to prepare for the communion service. As I started to set up the candles and the cup from my silver communion set on his tray table, Claude began to rouse. When I began the communion service, Claude followed along quite well and even repeated some of the words with me. As we, two disciples from Emmaus, shared the meal, both of us recognized Jesus again. Claude's eyes opened wide and became filled with light. The transformation was astonishing. After the Prayer of Thanksgiving, Claude beamed and exclaimed, "Well . . . thank you, thank you . . . this was wonderful!" By this time his whole face was full of light, and he had been restored to his full stature. No longer slumped in his chair, he now sat upright with his full attention focused on what was happening on his tray table.

I thought of Jesus' words: "Those who eat my flesh and drink my blood have eternal life, and I will raise them up on the last day; for my flesh is true food and my blood is true drink. Those who eat my flesh and drink my blood abide in me, and I in them."[35]

For Christians, our whole life takes shape and meaning from this meal with Jesus. Through eating and drinking we come to know who Jesus is. The bread and the wine nourish us into believing. "You are what you eat," Jesus seems to be saying. "When you eat and drink of me you become like me, you abide in me, you come to have life in me." That's the mystery of Jesus' life among us, a mystery we share as followers of the One who died and rose again.

Somehow the memory of this meal and its promise of salvation gave hope to Claude. His whole demeanor was restored. I cherish this final memory of Claude and think of him now at the heavenly banquet table surrounded by the saints in light.

PENTECOST

The Pentecost Spirit Comes!

For years we had put off painting and repairing the old windows in our church sanctuary. Many of them dated back to the colonial period and were now in a weakened condition. Some simply needed a good coat of paint—those were the modern windows—but the older colonial windows needed new muntins, a very costly project.

In looking around for a way to do this work inexpensively, the head of the church's property committee got in touch with a nonprofit agency at a local prison where the work could be done by inmates in the shop. So each window had to be carefully removed and taken to the prison, where the repairs were made and the window repainted. For nearly a year, one or more of the large sanctuary windows was missing. The openings were covered over with makeshift plywood frames and heavy plastic sheeting.

Those plastic covers gave us an exciting experience. In the middle of winter storms they kept popping out. Imagine trying to put that heavy plastic back in place during a storm. The covers turned into sails, with the wind filling them out. Once during worship, several strong gusts of wind whipped up, and everyone in the congregation shuddered. It seemed as if the temporary windows were going to pop open right during worship. The sensation was a bit like having the whole congregation sit in a large tent, the wind pushing against the flaps and threatening to blow over the whole fragile structure. Another interesting feature of these temporary window coverings was that you could easily hear the street noise in the church sanctuary, and conversely, you could hear the sound of the organ and the choir quite clearly outdoors.

When Pentecost came, it was not difficult to get the point of the story across. Everyone knew what it might have been like on that first Pentecost to hear the Holy Spirit come "like the rush of a violent wind."[36] Everyone knew the power in that wind and understood the frightening reaction the people might have had. Pop, there goes a window! Snap, there goes a temporary frame! There's no controlling what the wind will do next. It has a power all its own. So be it for the Holy Spirit! Imagine the strength the church would have if it could learn to move by the power of the Holy Spirit!

Pentecost Confusion

Pentecost Sunday, the birthday of the church. What a great festival it is! The Holy Spirit gives birth to the church fifty days after Jesus' resurrection. Now a new group of disciples is empowered by the Holy Spirit, ready to witness to the power of God at work in the life and death and resurrection of Jesus Christ. Scripture says they came "from every nation under heaven living in Jerusalem."[37] Though they all spoke different languages, they understood what was being said about God's deeds of power.

One Pentecost Sunday, however, our experience was more like the confusion of the Tower of Babel than the unity of that first gathering of Christians. That evening our church had agreed to host the opening banquet for the North American Maritime Ministries Association. People were indeed coming from all parts of North America, as well as England, and even the Vatican, for this meeting of people with responsibility for ministry to seafarers at major world ports. Philadelphia has a very active seamen's center just two blocks from our church, and this year, as they were the hosts of the gathering, we were asked to prepare and serve the meal in our social hall and hold the opening worship service in our sanctuary. Pentecost seemed like a great day to welcome these partners in ministry who are themselves so experienced in providing hospitality to people from around the world.

Normally we can fit about 120 people comfortably around the tables in our hall. But I saw that tables had been set for 150 persons. The tables had been pushed right up against the corners of the hall, and all the chairs we owned had been squeezed around them. The room looked great; the tables had been beautifully set, and flowers had been artfully arranged around the hall. Many church members had diligently worked to get everything ready, and there seemed to be more than enough people on hand to serve and to help with last-minute details. There was a spirit of cooperation and goodwill present in the room. As their pastor I was pleased by the teamwork I saw and proud of all the efforts at hospitality that were being made.

So I comfortably and confidently took a seat at one of the tables, with my back to the kitchen. I was engaged in a lively conversation with the people at my table, unaware of the chaos developing behind me. The cooks had miscalculated, and only *half* the food had been prepared. So half the guests were served and the other half had to wait and wait until their food was cooked. I began to wonder what the Holy Spirit was doing on this strange Pentecost Day. Everything had been turned upside down!

The task-oriented servers were becoming frustrated by their inability to do anything to change the situation, but the servers who had good relational skills were busy chatting and associating with our visitors from around the world. They were having a great time and kept everything lively. Fortunately our guests were very congenial and pleased just to be together and swap stories about their mutual concerns.

The final day of the three-day conference I met the person who had been the last to be fed that evening—the representative from the Vatican. He came over to greet me and tell me how much he enjoyed being at our church. I apologized for the lateness of his food, saying how embarrassed we were. "Never mind," he responded. "We were glad it happened to us. We all understood what was going on. The more important thing was that you opened your church to us—and your hearts."

Then I began to perceive some of what the Holy Spirit had been doing on that Pentecost evening. The Holy Spirit was reminding us that the relationships we have with one another are much more important than the work we do, that the intentions behind our actions are much more significant than whether we succeed or fail. The Holy Spirit had been present in a powerful way, teaching us and giving us new insight about the church and how we belong to one another through Jesus Christ. It had been a great Pentecost!

Lessons in Discipleship

The Pentecost season is called "ordinary time" and lasts almost half the year. But ordinary time can also be holy time when special occasions for learning in a personal, hands-on way are offered. Then Pentecost becomes a period for teaching about discipleship.

Most of the lectionary readings for this season are about the teaching and healing ministry of Jesus. For us at Old First it is the time when our teaching ministry swings into high gear. Especially during the month of June, young people from all over the country arrive to participate in our urban work camp program. They come, with their adult advisers, from as far away as Boston, St. Louis, Louisville, and rural Wisconsin.

As part of their week at the church and in the city, the youths volunteer at agencies offering services to homeless people. The locations include soup kitchens, drop-in centers, residences, shelters, and advocacy centers. At each agency, the young people do some sort of manual labor, such as a major cleanup, paint job, or repair project. As part of the program they get a chance to meet homeless people, work side by side with them, and listen to their stories. They also interact with the staff who are involved with the homeless on a full-time, long-term basis. It's surprising how much impact a week in the city can have on these impressionable young people, many of whom have never been in a large city. The exposure directly influences their career choices and vocational decisions and helps shape their vision of a Christian lifestyle in today's world.

Back at the church, the students have an opportunity to share their experiences with one another and reflect on their insights. Usually there is time for journaling and worship. It's incredible how many stereotypes get broken down when people have time to spend with one another and become acquainted on a very human level.

After spending several days in the city, the work campers are deeply affected by their experiences. Here are some of their comments.

"Because of my own naivete, I thought of homeless as a thing, a problem, but now I can put individual faces and warm personalities onto the word."—Jake

"Before this work camp I would be afraid of the homeless anytime I would go into Boston. I found out this week that the homeless are people that are not fortunate to own their own homes. This work camp experience helped me not to be afraid of homeless people. A lot of them are really friendly and caring."—Amy

"Chris and I were at St. Francis Inn, a soup kitchen on Kensington Avenue. The area around Kensington is probably the worst in Philadelphia. It has the highest rate of crime and drug use. Kensington is underneath an elevated train track, so even on the brightest day, it is dark in Kensington. It is a place you do not want to visit at night or in the day, for

that matter. St. Francis Inn . . . is like an oasis in a desert of despair.

"The people running St. Francis Inn are some of the best people I've ever met. They are accepting, kind, unselfish, and very friendly. They are willing to work from early in the morning until late at night with their only payment being a smile from someone they fed. When Chris and I were there they took us in like we had been there for years. By the end of the second day I felt comfortable enough to crack jokes.

"While giving out coffee and pastries in the morning a man that looked to be in his mid-forties came to the door and asked to use the bathroom. We let him in and pointed him towards the bathroom. He then motioned to someone who was not in our view. A small lady that looked to be in her seventies went to the bathroom instead. When I asked a guy who works at St. Francis Inn, he told me that somehow this man had lost everything he had and was out on the street. While trying to get enough money and food to survive, he was taking care of his mother. I hope that if confronted with the same situation, I could have as much love and dedication."—Geoff

"On arriving at Eliza Shirley House, a women's shelter, I was looking forward to trying almost anything. The task at hand was mindless busywork, making sandwiches and cleaning dishes. That was until the mad lunch rush. People came in by the dozens, mothers and children with faces that would tug at the heartstrings. I came around with food and drink. I smiled at the children and mothers as I would to any person I

cared about. If I didn't receive a thank-you, I would receive a smile or a look of gratitude.

"I cringed when I heard what the mothers were saying to their children. I was confused regarding the mothers' role. I was angry, thinking if you don't appreciate children, don't have them. It wasn't until later that I came to realize that homeless women are placed in all sorts of situations—evacuation, husbands running out on them, abuse, lack of education, becoming mothers at a young age. We arrived with questions and slowly began to understand the situation."—Elise

"I was brought closer to my true and inner self. I realize I want to do more with my life than make money. I want to help people. It doesn't necessarily mean working at a shelter, but doing something that directly or indirectly improves or enhances someone's life."—Lauren

"I'm now eighteen years old and am choosing the way I am going to live. Am I going to be a success by means of money, or by means of contentment with myself? Can I, someone coming from a well-off family, force myself to limit the luxuries and unnecessary opulence that I know I could get? Do I want to live a simple life? Would that life be so simple after all? I know I'd be happy and proud of myself, but society doesn't take well to this type of person. . . . All in all, the trip was a depressing eye-opener that will motivate me for the rest of my life to do things that make everyone a better person."—Nicole

It's amazing what can happen to young people during a week in the city. They arrive, ready and willing to serve others. They leave, helped by the very people they have come to serve. Somehow hearts are converted as homeless people and young people from the suburbs meet and find out how much they have in common. Lessons in discipleship—ultimately it's a process of people meeting people.

Christmas in July

Christmas in July? Yes, and in August too! Every day in the summertime is Christmas at Old First Reformed Church. While many churches nearly close down during the summer months because so many of their members are away, ours becomes even more active. Every corner of our building is in use.

We have a youth hostel nightly in our social hall, where we welcome young people from all over the world who are traveling. Some years we have had between six hundred and seven hundred young people spend the night during the weeks between the Fourth of July and Labor Day. And in the morning we serve breakfast to all the guests. When we advertise our youth hostel at the Tourist Center we say that we are more than a place to stay for a night. We are an active, historic presence in the city, and proceeds from the youth hostel help fund our summer outreach ministry to children and youth.

Every day, Monday through Friday, two vans leave our church headed ten blocks north, where, ever since the mid-1970s, we have operated a Tot Lot program for neighborhood children between the ages of five and eleven on a vacant property owned by the city. There a staff of four college-age students leads morning recreational activities, and in the afternoon they supervise trips to places of interest throughout the city.

A youth employment program to find jobs for teens in

businesses in our Center City neighborhood rounds out our summer program. We usually seek jobs for a dozen or so young people who receive orientation for their work assignments and are mentored during the summer by a church worker. This is the first opportunity many of these urban youths have at real employment. For most of them, jobs would not be available if the church did not go out and broker them. Sometimes, when the employer-employee relationship has gone well, the young people are able to keep their jobs during the school year.

The most intense learning of the summer occurs among the five or six students who form our summer staff and live in community in our church building. They get to try their hand at planning and carrying out activities with the children and youth. And they also have a rich experience of sharing space in a public building, learning about an urban environment, and getting acquainted with people from other countries and cultures. The summer staff usually comes from various parts of the United States and the world.

But how is *this* Christmas in July? Most people associate Christmas with carols and gift-giving and parties. What do all these summer activities have to do with the baby Jesus and the Christmas creche?

On the exterior, not much. But inside, something new comes to birth in each person through the activities and interaction of this outreach program. "In Christ," the apostle Paul tells us, "God was reconciling the world to God's self."[38] In Christ, God was creating a new humanity in which people care for one another and are gracious to one another. In Christ, we are being connected in positive, supportive ways. In essence our summer program is about relationships and relationship-building. In a culture based on individualism and in a city where life remains fairly anonymous, connecting people to one another in a responsible and creative way is something new. Welcoming foreign travelers to a place steeped in history and mission is something quite special. Following up on the many details of interpersonal interaction and using good communication skills to solve problems means taking the incarnation quite seriously.

The apostle Paul continues his exhortation: "So we are ambassadors for Christ, since God is making the appeal through us."[39] If the incarnation is to continue, we are the ones to carry on the work of reconciliation. Daily interaction with the children on the Tot Lot, comings and goings at the youth hostel, and encouraging and supporting youth in their employment opportunities provide the setting and occasion for Christ to be born, even in July.

Some of us were wondering how long Old First has been doing its summer outreach ministry in the city. We came across a news clipping from the summer of 1973 that noted a special celebration on the Tot Lot and included a photograph to support the facts of the story. There was Santa, clad in winter togs in the summer heat, asking a youngster what she wanted for Christmas. The summer program was getting a good start with Santa, simulated snow, and other trappings of Christmas. Perhaps the celebration was out of season, as the reporter noted, but it certainly was very much in keeping with the spirit behind our church's outreach ministry to children in the city.

Jazz 'n Berries

Strawberries, blueberries, peaches, cherries, apples—the seasons of our church year are punctuated with monthly food festivals. Originally they began as a way to raise money to pay off the mortgage on the restoration of our church building. It was one way our small congregation could work together to raise funds to meet those regular payments.

But even though the mortgage has been paid off, the festivals continue. Now the emphasis is on working together as a church family and interacting with our community. It is a way to invite people who live and work in our neighborhood to come inside our building for a meal and an opportunity to mix and mingle with others who also live and work in Center City.

Each festival attracts hundreds of people and is a great way for our guests to engage in the most basic activity of the life of a church—eating together! In addition, we've gained some wonderful free publicity for our church, as the festivals are announced in public-service spots on radio and TV and in the newspaper.

In June and July the parable of community extends into the evening as a jazz band provides the entertainment for what has come to be known as "Jazz 'n Berries." Sitting under the stars in front of our historic building, eating a big plate of blueberries and ice cream, and listening to the sounds of cool jazz is a good way to relax after a trying day at work. It is also our way of promoting community in the anonymity of the city, coaxing people who live in the large apartment buildings and condominiums around the church to come out and meet their neighbors. An impersonal city can be foreboding to newcomers, and the church can help break down the barriers by giving occasion for such simple values as friendship and neighborliness to blossom.

It's such an unassuming sign of openness and welcome and hospitality, yet city people need more and more safe places to gather and get acquainted. During intermission we talk about the history and mission of our church and invite people inside to see our beautiful sanctuary. The children especially enjoy the live music and lead us in having a good time.

Strawberries, blueberries, peaches, cherries, apples—all have their turn in the changing seasons of our church's life!

All Saints

Her name was Elizabeth. She was a blue-blooded Philadelphian who had been an illustrator of books and magazine articles. Elizabeth was homeless. She saw demons, heard voices, and out of these inner visions sketched drawings on the side of the box that served as a wall of her makeshift dwelling.

For years Elizabeth lived on the streets, wherever she could set up her lawn chair, carrying all her belongings in the shopping bags by her side. She spoke back to the voices within, but was oblivious to the world around her. It could be raining or quite chilly, Elizabeth didn't seem to be affected. She seemed captured by what was happening inside. If you tried to talk to her, she might snap back at you. She didn't want to be disturbed. Although she had a tough exterior, there was also something quite appealing about Elizabeth. If she appeared gruff and rough-edged on the outside, one look at her artwork, and you would be amazed by the refined pen-and-ink sketches and watercolors, drawn from her inner vision. She was able to capture the essence of her world with sensitivity and clarity.

Elizabeth was also a pioneer: she was the first homeless person to stay on our church premises for an entire winter season. In previous winters she had managed to keep warm by wearing several coats and sweaters and using cardboard boxes for protection from the elements; Elizabeth did not really want to come inside. Somehow she felt she would lose her independence indoors. Like most of us, Elizabeth treasured her independence. But her legs were developing infections, and she needed to bathe regularly.

The pastor of Old First at that time knew Elizabeth well, and after much coaxing persuaded her to set up her lawn chair in the entranceway to our church office. The boxes came along as well, and all her other worldly belongings—plastic dishes, tissues, paper towels, plastic bags, numerous small utensils, string, paper of all kinds, especially newspaper, and of course her pencils and pens.

There she was all winter long. Everyone who came to our church office—mail carriers, couples planning weddings, members of our church's official board, delivery persons, neighbors, monthly food festival workers—all got to know Elizabeth in one way or another. She might ignore these intrusions or snap back in a gruff voice. But no one could ignore Elizabeth's presence at our church.

In this way, Elizabeth became a pioneer. Because we got to know one homeless person and her circumstances intimately, church members and official board members were much more willing to allow other homeless people into our church building. Without knowing it, Elizabeth broke new ground and opened the door for many homeless people to come inside. The next summer, when she had made her way back to the streets of Philadelphia, Elizabeth was found dead under one of the bridges near the river.

On All Saints' Day we celebrate the pioneers of our faith. I think Elizabeth has earned a place among that company. I even believe she is in that great cloud of witnesses looking down upon our church as we continue to welcome the lost and the troubled into our lives.

The Reformation Continues

Tap, tap, tap. The year was 1517; the date, October 31, the eve of All Saints' Day. Political turmoil raged throughout Europe. The powers of evil had seemingly overtaken the church, and one uncompromising German monk was busily nailing something to the door of the church in Wittenberg.

Tap, tap, tap. "What are you doing? What are you putting up on that door, Brother Martin? What are you posting?"

"Oh, just a few theses. We clergy need to let the people know what is happening in our church these days. Some of the ideas of our leaders are threatening to undo us."

The discussion that followed was largely academic, but for Martin Luther the next years were very problematic. Having ignited a wholesale debate in the church, Luther had to defend his principles on every side. Finally in 1521 he was summoned to Rome to defend himself before Holy Roman Emperor Charles V, who declared Luther an outlaw, saying, "This devil in the habit of a monk has brought together ancient errors into one stinking puddle. . . . His teaching makes for rebellion, division, war, murder, robbery, arson, and the collapse of Christendom. He lives the life of a beast."[40]

Luckily Luther gained protection from the elector Frederick the Wise, who hid him in one of his castles, the Wartburg. There Luther was able to author a whole string of polemical pamphlets and to begin his translation of the Bible into German.

Tap, tap, tap. The year was 1967, and Owen Fox was busily nailing a placard to the doors of an abandoned paint warehouse at 330 Race Street in Center City, Philadelphia.

"Brother Owen, what are you doing? Why are you over here in Center City? I thought you lived in West Philadelphia? What are you nailing to the door of this ramshackle building?"

"Oh, just a zoning variance," Owen replied. "Our church in West Philadelphia has voted to come back here to restore this old building. It used to be our church. We built the building in 1774 and enlarged it in 1837—on the same site as our original building, which dated back to 1747. Our congregation is going to move back here and carry on a great ministry in this part of town."

You might think by Owen's determination that a large number of people were behind him, but church records reveal that fewer than one hundred congregants supported the move. It was a bold undertaking for a small congregation. And the new location was in a very down-at-the-heels part of town. In addition, prospects for the success of the relocation seemed grim. In fact, there was a published list of "Problems Related to the Relocation" that, like Luther's theses, was circulated widely.

Among the objections raised were the following:

• The area is already over-churched, and the two congregations currently located there receive support from their denominations for building maintenance and program.

• There are few residences in the area, and a ministry

to tourists or office workers will be hard to sustain and support.

• The Vine Street Expressway will be a natural barrier that will make it difficult to attract members from other parts of the city.

• The smaller the congregation becomes, the more difficult it will be to find capable leadership for church school and other activities.

• First Church does not have an endowment with which to support its building or specialized ministries for future generations.

So in 1967 the prospects of success in this new location seemed rather slim. But the congregation was willing to risk this move back to their roots. Church members were ready to step out onto what appeared to be very shaky ground. They seemed to have enthusiasm for this new venture. And that kind of risk-taking faith has made Old First Reformed Church unique over the years. Although it is an old historic church, the second oldest in continuous existence in the German Reformed tradition of the United Church of Christ, today it has a young, even pioneering attitude. Members are used to rolling up their sleeves and pitching in, whether it's to put up the shelter to stable farm animals for two weeks over the Christmas holidays, to open the church to house the homeless during the winter months, to give community activists a place to hold press conferences or gather for protest marches, to welcome visiting youth groups from around the country to participate in urban work camps, or to put on monthly food festivals to help pay for the restoration of the church building.

Recently the congregation completed its mortgage obligation on its historic building. What had once seemed insurmountable obstacles to the success of the church's ministry have been overcome. As part of the mortgage-burning celebration, many of the groups that had gotten their start in the building since 1967 were invited back. It was interesting to see how eager these groups were to return to worship with us. There were fifteen groups in all—civic organizations and musical organizations, members of Alcoholics Anonymous and homeless activists—many of whom had moved on to develop a life beyond our church. It was inspiring to realize how much energy had been birthed in our building and how that creativity had radiated out to encompass the whole city. The interesting aspect of our association with these groups is that we have a common history. We are written into their history, and they are written into ours.

The vitality of spirit present in the congregation today is a sign of hope for the future. Present members come from around the city and nearby suburbs, even crossing the river from New Jersey, to be part of a diverse urban congregation of various ages, races, sexual orientations, and ethnic groups that is not afraid to reach out into the community surrounding the church and to invite strangers in. In fact, the greatest challenge currently facing the church is lack of adequate facilities to accomplish all that the members want to do in the city.

In assembling the history of our church's return to its historic location in the 1960s, we discovered an interesting detail. A debate had raged in those early years over the need to install an elevator to make the second-floor church sanctuary accessible to persons with disabilities. It would be an expensive proposition. But eventually the congregation voted to put in the elevator. In excavating for the elevator shaft, the construction workers unearthed an old colonial well beneath the church's foundation. Just think—in reaching toward the future to make the sanctuary accessible to all, the church discovered an original treasure that had been hiding under its foundation over the centuries!

"Reformed and always reforming" was one of the rallying cries of the Reformation. We continue to need churches and church leaders who are willing to step out in faith and do bold and daring things in the community and in the world. It is easy, in the face of today's hard economic realities, to hold back and maintain the status quo. But more people are hungering and thirsting for the good news of Jesus Christ now than ever before, especially in our cities. May the Reformation continue, so that the church can move boldly into the next century with the commitment and conviction of its faith and a vision of engaging the world in creative and challenging ways. Who knows? We might unearth even more treasures from our past to delight and sustain us and to keep the surprising grace of Christmas alive through the years!

Notes

1. Mark 1:2–3a.

2. Meister Eckhart, from Matthew Fox, *Original Blessing* (Santa Fe: Bear and Co., 1983), 106.

3. Paraphrase of Luke 3:3 and Mark 1:4.

4. Luke 21:26.

5. Mark 13:33.

6. Matthew 24:40.

7. Romans 13:11b (RSV).

8. Anthony de Mello, "Presence," from *One Minute Wisdom* (Garden City, N.Y.: Doubleday and Co., 1985), 12.

9. Kenneth Grahame, *The Wind in the Willows* (New York: Dell Publishing, 1969), 91.

10. J. Barrie Shepherd, "The Silent Seers," from *The Moveable Feast* (Swarthmore, Pa.: The Sheepfold Press, 1990), 23.

11. John 1:29.

12. Matthew 1:18.

13. Matthew 1:19.

14. Matthew 1:20.

15. Ann Weems, "Getting to the Front of the Stable," from *Kneeling in Bethlehem* (Philadelphia: Westminster Press, 1980), 50.

16. A conversation with Tim Schramm on Acts of Thomas, 39.

17. Galatians 2:19b–20.

18. Howard Thurman, "The Work of Christmas," from *The Mood of Christmas* (Richmond, Ind.: Friends United Press, 1973), 23.

19. Luke 2:29–32.

20. Meister Eckhart, from a sermon in *Breakthrough: Meister Eckhart's Creation Spirituality in New Translation*, introduction and commentary by Matthew Fox (New York: Image Books, 1980), 330.

21. "I Wonder As I Wander," Appalachian carol, by John Jacob Niles, copyright 1934 by G. Schirmer, Inc., as used in *The Hymnal of the United Church of Christ* (Philadelphia: United Church Press, 1974), no. 119.

22. *The Sunday Bulletin*, 3 March 1977, 14.

23. Luke 2:35.

24. 1 Corinthians 1:18, 20b, 25.

25. Paraphrase of Mark 15:39b.

26. Paraphrase of Mark 15:31b–32a.

27. See 1 Corinthians 1:25.

28. Matthew 11:28–29.

29. Thomas Merton, *Raids on the Unspeakable* (New York: New Directions, 1966), 70, 72.

30. Isaiah 53:2–3a.

31. Nicola Slee, "Spring Trees at Pleshey," from *New Christian Poetry*, ed. Alwyn Marriage (London: Collins, 1990), 120–21.

32. John 15:4.

33. "O Sons and Daughters of the King," by Jean Tisserand, trans. John M. Neale, as used in *The Hymnal of the United Church of Christ* (Philadelphia: United Church Press, 1974), no. 135.

34. Mark 16:7.

35. John 6:54–56.

36. Acts 2:2b.

37. Acts 2:5b.

38. Paraphrase of 2 Corinthians 5:19a.

39. Paraphrase of 2 Corinthians 5:20a.

40. Roland H. Bainton, *Here I Stand* (New York: Mentor Books, 1950), 147.